One

ELEVEN O'CLOCK AT NIGHT. A young man drives through a snowstorm, eastward on Interstate 64. He's midway between St. Louis and Oxford, Ohio. It is late November. The storm was unexpected.

The young man is a first-year graduate student supported by a full scholarship at Miami University. The storm frightens him.

His car's a yellow VW bug with a ragtop that ripples in his windy speed. The weather's cold enough to freeze his feet. Soft snow has sifted inside and pillows his shoes at the floorboard.

What frightens him most are the snowflakes— huge, globular. His headlights illuminate them in the distance where they fall like a curtain, softly. Closer to the car, however, the thick flakes level and fly at his windshield, exploding like missiles.

This fusillade is the personal assault of a malicious world.

Until this particular day, the firmament, the earth, the sun, the moon, the clouds, and all creation had been a world in which he was a citizen. The spirit of God blew through it. The love of God had made it.

But now, as far as the young man is concerned, God is absent.

The seventh seal of the scroll in the eighth chapter of the book of Revelation has been broken open, and now there is a vast silence in heaven, and the grounded wind howls. This strafing of the snow, and his fear before it, bears witness that the young man has lost his faith.

THREE DAYS AGO THIS young man arrived at Concordia Seminary seeking not only the companionship of old friends, but also a confirmation of the faith he fears is running from his soul like sand through a rip in a bag.

The class he went to visit had been his own class through high school and college. They'd attended an all-male boarding school which prepared boys, youth, and young men for the Christian ministry—six years together, they had been: from fourteen years to nineteen, a very long time to live in camaraderie. But after graduating six months ago, the young man had decided not to go Concordia Seminary with the others; instead, he diverged to Miami University, in Oxford, Ohio.

So he went to his old, faithful family, thinking that

he might find comfort and assurance. But his class was busy about their personal affairs. They acknowledged his presence. They greeted him happily—but then went off in other directions. Randy Graur had a new girlfriend. Roger Stuenkel had broken up with his and was looking for another. In the half-year since they'd parted ways, his old classmates had changed. Or he had changed. He and they lived in separate spheres.

While at the seminary, the young man attended chapel. But the preacher that morning preached about some pillar of the church who died a century ago. The church, therefore, seemed walled within itself. He was but a knocker outside the door.

So now he drives back to Oxford unaccompanied, and the violent snowflakes scorn him.

He does not doubt that the Creator still exists somewhere in the empyrean, but that he had abandoned his people long ago and left them to their own devices.

I am, of course, that young man.

Two

UNTIL I DEPARTED FOR GRADUATE school, my whole education was devoted to preparing me to be a pastor in the Lutheran Church.

Now I was beginning to realize that my school had been an encasement, and that that encasement itself had been the shape and unconscious proof of my faith. A jello mold is the shape of the jello within it. But it is not the jello. The rituals, the lessons, the school's history—the mold, you see, of my spirit while I still dwelled in them—were the forms that kept me from ever questioning the reality of Christian faith.

We boys attended chapel every morning, five times a week. On Saturdays there was no chapel, but on Sundays we went to churches where we sang Christian hymns, heard the tenants of faith preached, and taught the Sunday school children the established Lutheran doctrine. We, of course, taught what we had learned.

The chapel walls declared faith by the symbols painted there and in the Latin that Martin Luther used: "Sola Gratia," "Sola Fide," "Sola Scriptura"—Grace alone, Faith alone, Scriptures alone.

We studied the Old and the New Testaments. We to learned to speak and to read German and Latin and Greek. Our professors were ordained ministers, most with pastoral experience. We obeyed a strict schedule, studying for two hours before the evening lights went out and we were to be in bed. Proctors were appointed to check on our obedience. Most orderly were our days.

Concordia was an all-male school. My room was on the third floor of a dormitory built in 1881: #314 Wunder Hall—three roommates, four desks, two bunk beds. If we committed some infraction (like missing chapel), we were commanded to do *Strafarbeit* for a certain period of time. *Strafarbeit:* "punishment-work."

Men and boys were raucous in the hallways and on the playing fields. Upperclassmen had power over their inferiors, whom they commanded to make their beds, push with their noses wet gum across the floors, and foot-race around cinder ovals—the loser to receive whacks from a paddle.

The classes were named by a count of Latin numerals: Sexties, freshmen; Quintas, sophomores; Tertsionors, juniors, Quartoners, seniors; Secundas, freshmen college students; Primoners, sophomores in college.

Once, in the swimming pool dressing room, two

upperclassmen came to me and asked me to judge a contest. The first fellow hit me on my shoulder. The second one took his turn: boom! "Who," they asked, "hit you the harder?" If I dared to pick one man over the other, the other demanded a rematch.

Benny Ason jumped from the loft of a barn and landed on a pitchfork. His bung-hole was huge ever thereafter.

One of my roommates defied the laws both of the school and the state by fermenting apple juice in his closet. Moreover, he filled Listerine bottles with whiskey and sold them to schoolmates. He had scratched the mortar around a cinder block in one of the walls until the block came out. Then he hid the whiskey bottles in the cavity behind it. When one of the proctors got wind of his enterprise, my poor roommate collected all the bottles in a gym bag, climbed to the roof of the dorm, and threw the bag as far as he could. It crashed against a parapet. But he was found out nonetheless and quickly expelled.

Were these hijinks matters of faith? Indeed they were—at least the form of it. For shagging and hazing imposed a formal order upon the students not unlike the Great Chain of Being. It prepared them for the hierarchy that would govern the church thereafter. It established an intimate brotherhood, not only brother with brother, but also with the generations of pastors who had gone before.

My father and my grandfather, my great-grandfather and my great-great-grandfather had attended these same institutions. Four generations of Wangerins. They all became ministers, each convinced of his vocation. My great-grandfather spent his whole pastorate at a single parish in Illinois.

What chance had I to do otherwise? I walked where the saints had trod.

ALREADY FROM MY BIRTH was I shapen in the faith.

On the first page of a baby book entitled *Life Begins,* my father inscribed his expectations for my vocation— the ministry, which was his own vocation and, he assured himself, would also be mine.

In black block letters he printed the scriptures of his assurance:

> *For this child I prayed; and the Lord hath given me my petition which I asked of him. Therefore also I have lent him to the Lord. As long as he* (as long as my father's son) *liveth, he shall be lent to the Lord.*

My father, ever assiduous for details, added the Scriptural reference: *"1 Samuel 1:27-28."*

Throughout my first year, Walter Sr. continued to

write the Bible verses according to which he planned to raise me:

> *"Lo, children are an heritage of the Lord: and the fruit of my womb is his reward."*
> —*Psalm 127:3*

> *"As newborn babes, desire the sincere milk of the word, that you may grow thereby."*
> —*1 Peter 2:2*

> *"But grow in grace, and in the knowledge of our Lord and our Savior Jesus Christ. To him be glory now and forever. Amen."*
> —*2 Peter 3:18*

> *"He that believeth and is baptized shall be saved. But he that believeth not shall be damned."*
> —*Mark 16:16*

Believing brought salvation. Believing not brought damnation.

What if I should cease to believe?

Theologies built the spiritual house in which I grew. A child doesn't question air. He breathes it. He doesn't question the religious atmosphere or the religious devotion of his parents. He abides in them. They constitute his cosmos.

Moreover, we can trace the line of our heritage back to "Stadt Wangerin" in the Prussia of 1750, to a shepherd named Johann Friedrich Wangerin—so faithful that when fire burnt down his superior's farm, Johann proudly announced that he had not lost one of his sheep. Generation after generation of faithful Lutherans.

Why, then, would I *not* consider myself a Christian? Faith was my casement. Faith was my father's house. Faith made that house a pastor's parsonage.

Now I lay me down to sleep.
I pray the Lord my soul to keep.
If I should die before I wake,
I pray the Lord my soul to take.

So my parents prayed with their children about life and death. And if the day had been marred by some transgression, my mother prayed with us (sometimes with fervor) the prayer that begged forgiveness:

Jesus, Savior, wash away
All that has been wrong today.
Help me every day to be
Good and gentle, more like thee.

When I was about ten, the Reverend Walter Wangerin Sr. began to wear a black shirt with a white clerical collar. He said that, like a policeman's uniform, this was his way of indicating his vocation even to strangers.

Dad smoked Camel cigarettes in a cigarette stem. This, he said, was to keep his fingers from smelling of tobacco smoke when he laid the communion wafer on a communicant's tongue. Likewise, he would scratch half-moons of soap under his fingernails: a sweet-smelling aroma in case some scent of the cigarette still lingered despite his caution. When he was thirty-two he suddenly gave up smoking. He put his last two packs in our freezer. One year later he gave them to a boarder in our parsonage. They were still fresh.

When he preached, elaborating the faith with a powerful rhetoric, building walls of the Christian creeds, his family sat in the front pew of the sanctuary.

"Wally," said the congregation, "you are the spitting image of your father."

Walter Sr. had a high forehead. Above that he combed his hair into a rakish loop, a handsome man. He entertained the youth group (called, in those days, the Walther League) by playing a sly piano, and the Walther League youth sang with gusto. Reverend Walter Sr. wrote short chancel dramas in which members of the Sunday school took various roles. These plays were milked for the radios of city-dwellers and farmers.

Once, when the play enacted the Passion of Christ, Don Affeldt, an eighth-grader playing Judas, flung a handful of washers across the stones of the chancel, and all we children screamed, "Crucify him! Crucify him!"

On Sunday mornings, between the services, my father wore a black cassock, its black buttons buttoned from his throat to the toes of his shoes. During the worship service itself he donned a white surplice, and over the surplice a stole hung round his neck. These were the more glorious trappings of his ministry, the garments of his vocation. And the father expected his son so to dress, the son who knew nothing of his future except that his father's vestments would one day vest him too.

The sanctuary of Emmanuel Lutheran Church in Grand Forks, North Dakota, was of brick painted an ivory white. Arched dark beams supported the ceiling. The furniture of the chancel was blonde and intricately carved. Stained glass windows watered the interior with blue pools and green and red. Chandeliers hung from the beams on long, strong metal chains, swaying slightly, when Wally watched them, under heaven.

Walter Jr. abided in this house of the Lord.

Then there came the year when I thought I had lost Jesus.

Everyone else moved through the church with a blithe unconcern. No one was anguished but me. The people knew what I did not: that God was in his holy temple and all was right in the world. Surely they knew where Jesus walked in Emmanuel Lutheran Church.

But I had never actually seen him there—or anywhere else.

Therefore I sought him everywhere. During worship I troubled my mother by dropping down to the floor and peering under the pews. Two hundred human feet, but Jesus wasn't there.

When my father chanted the liturgy facing the altar, the baritone voice that filled the sanctuary seemed too splendid to be his. It must be Jesus chanting! After worship I crept up the chancel steps to look behind the wooden altar, which was a box shaped something like a casket. The back of the altar lacked a side. There was dust. There were old hymnals. But there was no Jesus.

I was expecting the Lord to be wandering somewhere in a woolen robe cinched with a rope at his waist. He would wear sandals and walk with a shepherd's staff. His hair would fall in waves to his shoulders. I'd know him when I saw him.

There was one room in the church building I had never entered. One Sunday I took courage between my teeth, slipped from the pew on a pretext of peeing, and went downstairs to the women's bathroom. Holy, holy, holy was that secret place.

My heart pounded as hard as John Henry's hammer.

Timidly I pushed the door open.

"Jesus? Are you in here?"

I went fully inside. There was a beautiful counter

and a large mirror on the wall behind it and a stool set before it. These may have been a wonder to behold. But as yet no Jesus. No one at all. Jesus must be hiding in the toilet stall. Slowly I nudge the stall door open. No one, not even Jesus, was sitting on the pot.

I returned to my mother desolated.

You wouldn't say I had lost my faith. I scarcely knew what faith *was*. But I felt abandoned. I was the loneliest kid to have been cast out of the sweet communion of the saved.

Communion.

Dad in his other-worldly voice, "In the night in which he was betrayed, our Lord took bread, broke it, blessed it, and gave thanks. He gave it to his disciples, saying, 'Take and eat. . . .'"

Shortly, people began to line up in the aisle. My mother rose and joined them.

I watched her go as if for the first time. She kneeled on a cushion before the low rail—and I was horrified.

My mother was a mighty woman, strong of arm and sturdy in her opinions. She it was who ruled our household. Once, when we were camping in Glacier National Park, a great bear came out of the woods: *Ursus Horribilis*. It stood up on its hind legs and twitched its wet, black nostrils, sniffing the air. It dropped to all fours. The creature began to shuffle toward our tent. As if she were a bear before another bear, my mother picked up a pan and a spoon and stalked forward, banging the pan and hollering, "Get out! Run, boomer! You have no business here!" It wasn't my mother who backed down.

Yet now, in church, she seemed to do what she'd never done before. The woman *knelt* at the communion rail. Moreover, humbly she let my father feed her. He didn't just hand her the cracker, but put it directly upon her tongue! Next he tipped the rim of a cup to her lips, and she drank.

When she walked back to our pew, my mother's head was bowed as meekly as one of her children. In this manner she sat down beside me—her head lowered, her eyes closed, her hands folded, breathing through her nose.

I smelled mystery on her breath.

"Mommy, what's that?"

"Hush!"

"I mean, what's that in your mouth?"

"Wine."

"No, but what's that *in* you?"

"Oh," she said. "It's Jesus."

No robe. No rope. No sandals. But the Spirit of the Christ. All along Jesus had been hiding inside my mother. Here was a wonder I could scarcely understand. But my mother had said it. It must be true.

WHEN I WAS TEN years old, my father accepted a call to become the president of a Lutheran Junior College in Edmonton, Alberta, Canada.

He told me that such calls came from the Holy Spirit.

This junior college prefigured the college I would inhabit four years later. The forms of faith were, apparently, everywhere. And I did my Christian duty.

I felt constrained to announce to my teachers that God had created the world in six days, and on the seventh he rested.

I told Jimmy Demos that he should not pray to saints, or else he would not enter heaven.

At the appointed age I attended confirmation classes. I memorized whole chunks of the Bible. Even today I can recite the confirmation verse which I chose as my own for life:

Ask and it shall be given unto you.
Seek and you shall find.
Knock and it shall be opened unto you.

There were four of us in the class: two boys, Greg and me; and two Dutch sisters more interested in Greg than in memorizing or in me. Under pressure from my mother, and watched as the first son of President Wangerin, I worked very hard. I memorized not only Bible passages, but also the commandments together with Martin Luther's explanation of every command-ment.

The first commandment:

Thou shalt have no other gods before me.

What does this mean?

We should fear, love, and trust in God above all things.

The second:

Thou shalt not take the name of the Lord thy God in vain.

What does this mean?

We should fear and love God that we may not curse, swear, use witchcraft, lie, or deceive by his name, but call upon it in every trouble, pray, praise, and give thanks.

The third:

Remember the Sabbath day to keep it holy.

What does this mean?

We should fear and love God that we may not despise preaching and his word, but hold it sacred and gladly hear and learn it.

And so forth and so on.

On the day of my confirmation, we were examined first before the whole congregation. Though the other three maundered through poor efforts at memory, I recited every word perfectly.

As a present and congratulation for my formal acceptance into the church, my aunt gave me my first Bible with gilt-edged pages and the Lord Christ's words printed in red.

Was this my own true faith? My own fearing and loving and trusting in the Almighty Father? Not really. It was *the* faith, that which I could deliver word for word. A static thing. I had learned *about* the commandments and the creed of the Church. I believed they were true—as I believed the stars are true. But I did not cling to this creed. Rather, I wore it like a badge. My father's son on his way to fulfilling my father's dreams.

If, however, you asked me then if I had faith, I would brightly answer, "I do."

I had a paper route that took me to the edge of the city. This far north, darkness descended before three o'clock in the afternoon. When it snowed I would stand at the extreme end of my route and stare across a wide, snowy truck-parking lot. The sight was soft and empty and very sad.

It was as if the universe had nothing to say. A premonition. Perhaps my feelings were a premonition of the absence of my God.

FINALLY, IT WAS IN the snows of Oxford, Ohio, when all the trappings and the external forms of faith no longer acted as the shape that shaped my soul, that I learned that to believe *in* something—as opposed to believing something *about* something—was not my truth after all. Not the truth of a personal trust.

Three

"THERE ARE FINALLY TWO FORMS of loneliness that cannot either be covered or escaped," wrote Paul Tillich in *The Eternal Now*:

> . . . *the loneliness of guilt and the loneliness of death. Nobody removes from us that which we have committed against our true being. We feel both our hidden guilt and our open guilt as* ours, *and ours alone. . . . We are alone with it. And it is a loneliness that permeates all other forms of loneliness, transforming them into experiences of judgment.*

I took up lodging in a single-room efficiency apartment on Oxford's Main Street. It had a tiny bathroom and a tinier kitchen. I drank port and smoked a pipe in order to soothe my restlessness and ease my profound homesickness.

I slept on my father's old army cot, worked at the ancient oak desk that had been his, and typed on an Underwood typewriter, circa 1920. That, too, had been my father's. I listened to an inexpensive record player (Brahm's 2nd symphony, my favorite album). And, of course, I cooked for myself.

Miami was a gracious old campus.

When I walked the streets before going to bed, its lamps shed a poor light but added an old-world atmosphere to the sidewalks. In autumn the skittering of dry leaves sounded like children behind me. There was a stone bench behind the Episcopal church upon which I would sit. Apart from my studies, my mind fingered sorrows.

I had determined to write a poem a day. In those days I sought to become a significant poet.

Come to me, all ye who labor and are heavy laden,
  and I will give you rest.

There was a Lutheran church in Hamilton, Ohio, about sixteen miles southeast of Oxford. I worshipped there during September, but stopped for the flimsiest of reasons. A thick-necked man sang every hymn in an outrageously loud tenor voice. I considered him a show-off. He irritated me. And the pastor, when he invited me to a Sunday dinner, seemed much more interested in his stereo system (which, he said, he'd built himself) than in ministry.

My first classes were Shakespeare's tragedies, Old English, the principles of research—and a seminar with a professor whom I despised immediately.

He paced around the long, single table in the room offending his students by a foul, whining mouth. He frequently referred to "limp penises," as he said it, and, more outrageously, "dry cunts."

I distinguished myself by approaching Dean Spiro Peterson and demanding to switch to a different class.

Dr. Peterson granted me my request.

Once, after my departure, the offensive professor saw me chatting with a young woman. He approached us like an unhappy dog and said, "You're talking about me, aren't you!"

Still in autumn I would drive to a state park in Kentucky and walk and walk its grounds, allowing my loneliness to feel like a sweet suffering.

When I read each new poem in the morning, I found to my dismay that it was stupid and overblown. By Thanksgiving I'd begun to doubt the possibility of my dream. No poem was not a failure.

I bought a single-shot twenty-two rifle, then often visited a shooting range to train myself in accuracy. In this I did prevail. I could toss a tin can into the sky and pot it before it hit the ground.

When I entered graduate school I'd expected to earn grades below those of the other students. Well, I'd come from a college of less than two hundred men, while the others had come from big state schools. But Concordia had grounded me in an excellent education. My Old English professor chuckled as he returned one test, saying that Wangerin alone had gotten every answer right, declensions and conjugations and vocabulary. German had prepared me. And I received nothing less than A's during the next two years. I took comfort in my performance. I took comfort anywhere I could get it.

One of my classmates, a Texan, regularly smoked pot. He tried to persuade me to join him. I didn't. Not because I considered myself of a higher morality than his, but because I feared its effects.

There was an older woman in our class. Just before she'd come to Miami she'd gotten a divorce. My pot-smoking friend went to her and offered himself to relieve her sexual tensions.

She refused the offer. I thought it was because of her ethical standards, but it wasn't. She told me that she had appreciated the young man's empathy.

This was not the world in which I'd grown up.

On the other hand, my Texas friend would often knock on my door late at night. He was continually depressed and hoped to find some solace in my religiosity. I explained as much as I could, but failed—perhaps because I only believed that I believed the solutions I mouthed.

Soon he was making it with a woman who lived with her brother outside Oxford. One afternoon they drove past me in a jeep with flowers painted on its sides. My friend pointed at me, said something in the woman's ear. They both threw back their heads in laughter— and I was now the professor of foul language. "They are talking about me!"

There was the high stump of a tree in front of my apartment. The tree itself must have been twisted off in some windstorm, for the top fibers of the trunk were wrenched in what seemed to me an agony of grief. The convulsion made me very sad.

> *Only the righteous shall go into the house of the Lord.*

Sadness did indeed attend me on my midnight walks.

It was now, some weeks before I drove to St. Louis, that I felt I was losing hold on my Christian faith.

Shakespeare wrote his tragedies in the assumption of an orthodox faith. Claudius, the king of Denmark, suffering the guilt of his sins, prays for forgiveness:

> *Try what repentance can. What can it not?*
> *Yet what can it when one can not repent?*
> *O wretched state! O bosom black as death!*
> *O liméd soul, that struggling to be free*
> *Art more engaged! Help, angels! Make assay.*
> *Bow, stubborn knees, and heart with strings of steel,*

Be soft as sinews of the new-born babe.
All may be well.

And so the king bows himself in silent prayer.

Hamlet enters and believes that Claudius is purging his soul. Hamlet is convinced of heaven and of the prayers of confession:

O, such a deed
As from the body of contraction plucks
The very soul, and sweet religion makes
A rhapsody of words. Heaven's face does glow,
O'er this solidity and compound mass
With tristful visage, as against the doom,
Is thought-sick at the act.

Hamlet means the act of killing the king at his prayers. Hamlet (Shakespeare?) is convinced of the efficacy of prayer and repentance. Why not I?

Because King Claudius fails at his confession too:

My words fly up, my thoughts remain below:
Words without thoughts never to heaven go.

And I was worse than the king because I could not pray with sincerity, could not pray faithfully, could not pray at all.

It scared me. Therefore I tried to prove my faith by

putting three questions to myself, catechetical questions.

Walking toward the stone bench behind the Episcopal church, I asked:

"Do you believe that there was a Christ on earth?

And I answered, "Yes."

"Do you believe that Jesus died on a cross?"

"Yes."

"Do you believe that Jesus rose again?"

This was difficult. I spent time before I answered it. Then, gritting my teeth and blanking my mind against historical realities, I said, "Yes."

I walked back to my apartment having satisfied myself—on the surface.

On the surface, I say, because the confession was weaker than my doubt. Doubt was a roaring lion. Faith was a lamb.

After the snowstorm between St. Louis and Oxford, I searched myself with a terrible honesty and found the axioms of my soul's genuine beliefs.

I sinned. That was flat, because I suffered a persistent guilt. But I sinned against people, not against the God who had absconded. And *this* I knew because to ask God for forgiveness was easy and abstract. And if there was forgiveness in him, I had no proof of it. On the other hand, to approach the person against whom I had sinned, and to confess that sin, was a painful humiliation. Nor could I trust in her forgiveness, and what then? Guilt would never be assuaged. But her forgiveness, *that* could set me free.

For my well-being, a single human person was profoundly more valuable than God.

Again, I didn't think that there was no God. God existed. But the more I thought on him, the more I came to these conclusions:

If God was the Infinite, he had only to be, and his infinitude would crush me with the recognition of my finitude. Limitlessness proves the limitedness of the entire universe; and within that universe galaxies are small whirlpools, and I am but an infinitesimal speck.

I thought of it this way: Let's say that God is sleeping on some hyper-celestial bed. He turns over. His arm flops out. That arm beats me silly, and God is completely unaware of what he has done to me.

God dreams, and what he dreams *is*. I can dream. I can hope, for example, to be a great poet. But *my* dreams are abstractions. They may never be realized. Nothing assures their realization. I can imagine my success. I can hope. But I cannot actually succeed, and hope is merely chimerical.

Witness my poetical nighttime efforts—how they are by morning failures. God knows nothing of failure. How, then, could he know my desolations?

Morality is more a human characteristic than a godly one.

All of this made me angry at God.

Where are the proofs, except my frustrations?

Four

M Y FATHER NEVER GOT OVER the miserable way he was treated by the faculty and much of the college board during his tenure as president of Concordia College in Edmonton, Canada.

He dealt with angry and open complaints. One member of the faculty had expected to be appointed president before Walter Wangerin Sr. had. That seed of jealousy sprouted in a number of hearts. The faculty women, so my mother was convinced, gossiped about her. She could cut them no more than cut a horde of flying hornets. She felt ostracized. I can't tell you now the accusations they leveled at my parents, but I saw their bloodied souls.

In the end, dad was forced to resign.

He had had dreams. I think he hoped to find a seat at synodical headquarters. But after his departure his dreams were all deflated.

I remember the day we drove from Edmonton for the last time. As we passed a cemetery, my father suddenly pulled to the side of the street, leaped out of the car with his camera, and dodged into the cemetery. He took a picture. He did not tell us of what. But after he furnished his new office in Chicago, the photograph appeared on his filing cabinet. It was of a tombstone. On the stone was carved the name of his most aggressive enemy, the man from whom my father had stolen the presidency.

Dreams fall to naught. Even the Lord God to whom he prayed had not answered his prayers, and he, my father, carried the wound unto his death.

In old age he would repeat passionately the story of his defeat. When he came to the climax he would slap my leg as if I were a table and shout his displeasure.

I DROVE HOME FOR Christmas.

Our family's rituals had never varied throughout the years. Dad bought the Christmas tree on the twenty-third of December. There were two reasons for the tardiness of his purchase.

1. Trees were cheaper then.

2. He always said that Advent, the days before Christmas, were *not* Christmas! The celebration could not, should not, start until the eve of the holy day—and

that *after* the pageant had been performed at church.

Moreover, though dad would himself trim the tree on the twenty-third (always hanging one silvery tinsel at a time so that each would dangle straight down), he would then remove the knob from the door of that room lest any child might sneak a peek and spoil the schedule. This was in the early days, before we left Edmonton.

Then his sons and daughters put on their pajamas and lined up in the kitchen, where dad would preach a short sermon and lead us in singing the thirteenth verse of Luther's hymn, "From Heaven Above to Earth I Come."

Ah, dearest Jesus, holy child,
Make thee a bed soft, undefiled,
Within my heart that it may be
A quiet chamber kept for thee.

After that we would follow him through the mystery-door and find our mother sitting on the floor beside the tree, her skirt a great swirl around herself. The only lights in the room were the Christmas tree lights, casting their colored glory on the walls and on the face of our mother. Beside her were seven piles of presents, one for each of the children.

But after we'd taken up residence in Chicago, these rituals had been forsaken. Christmas was much more prosaic.

I bought my mother a set of green drinking glasses. I don't remember that they were ever used.

I feared that one of my siblings would burst into tears. Heightened expectations can so easily be disappointed. Teasing destroyed my sister's composure. Two of my brothers suffered the scorn of their schoolmates, and one of these was broken by his inability to make good grades. He couldn't read, but neither the teachers nor our mother knew the term "dyslexia."

Dad spent most of his time in his office.

Mom was unhappy.

I came home lonely. I took loneliness back with me to Oxford.

My scholarship—a National Defense Fellowship awarded by the United States government itself—had spared me the duties of teaching during the first term.

Now it was the second term. Besides my own studies, I was to instruct two classes of college freshmen in the various forms of written compositions. The students were required to read the essays of well-known authors as examples of good form and then once a week, every week, try to imitate what they had read.

I prepared to teach the initial class by writing several pages of notes. These I laid on a lectern. I never moved from the lectern.

The class was to last an hour and a quarter. Well, I zipped through my notes so fast that I was done in forty-five minutes. Despite the wintry day, my armpits were dark with sweat. And I had absolutely nothing else to say.

So I dismissed the class, and beat them out the door, and fairly ran to a small cafe, and drank a hundred cups of coffee.

No teacher, I. I couldn't remember a single student's face. I don't think I had raised my eyes to look at them.

My one-room apartment was on the second floor of a house that used to serve one family.

Across the hall was a newly-married couple. They would greet me on the landing at the top of the stairs. Sometimes we chatted. They hated Lyndon Baines Johnson. I liked him, especially for his passage of the Civil Rights Act. But I did not defend him against the married couple's attacks. They were not much educated. I was. Nevertheless, I feared to offend even these mere acquaintances.

In January a hellish homesickness overcame me. I could not understand why.

My actual home had little to offer. Whenever I drove to Chicago, the sight of the massive Calumet granaries tore at my heart. They were symbols of the sorrow I would meet when I got home.

I might have been homesick for the college and the friends of my past. But my visitation had wiped that home out. Perhaps I yearned for my past. For child-hood? For the wide prairies of North Dakota—the flashes of Eden? No, that wasn't enough to explain the dark pit into which I had been thrown. And childhood had been replaced by the long confusions that clouded the house before I reached my thirteenth year.

Now, so many decades after graduate school, I am able to say what I could not then: I had become a solitary wanderer in the universe. The world-rim walker.

> *The weary-hearted may not withstand fate, nor*
> *the torn spirit bring help . . .*
> *So I, often wretched with care, deprived of my*
> *homeland, far from dear kinsmen, had*
> *to fasten my heart's thought with fetters.*
> *Downcast I crossed over the woven waves,*
> *winter-sad, yearning for a hall . . .*
> *He who has felt it knows how cruel a companion is*
> *sorrow to him who has no beloved protectors.*
> *The path of exile attends him. Frozen are the*
> *thoughts in his heart-case, no joy on earth . . .*
> *Sorrow and sleep bind the poor lone-dweller.*

Five

WHEN WE HAD ENTERED THE United States again from Canada, we stopped for a day or two in Portland, Oregon. I had been born as the first of my parents' seven children, born at 7:00 p.m. in a suburb called Vanport. Now my father and I stood on a ridge overlooking Vanport.

My father had told members of his congregation that if at my baptism I cried lustily, his son would surely become a preacher.

After the baptism, the elders approached him with faces "as long as hoe-handles."

He asked them, "What's the matter."

They said, "The baby didn't make the first peep."

Vanport was built on a perfect grid of straight streets at ninety-degree angles to one another. The navy had a shipyard there. Sailors flocked to his church.

So now my father and I gazed down on what used to be Vanport. It was summer. The sight was almost violent with sunlight. And all its houses were gone. Only the flat grid remained. Weeds grew in the gaps.

The world would not stand still. The places that humans abandoned, nature took back for herself. All was lost.

Before that summer was done, my mother, Virginia Storck Wangerin, bought me new underwear. She packed my clothes in an aluminum box. Then she and my father drove me north from Chicago to Milwaukee, where I was enrolled, fourteen years of age, at Concordia. The school rules prevented me from visiting home, or even telephoning. On the trip south to Chicago for the Thanksgiving holiday, I saw patches of snow in the cornfields. My sisters and brothers, too, were lost to me.

I happened upon a book entitled *Crime and Punishment.* I followed that with Dostoevsky's *The Brothers Karamazov.* Next I read the fat novel *Look Homeward, Angel,* which gave a name to my place in the Wangerin household:

> *O, lost, and by the wind grieved, ghost come back again.*

I read a play by Christopher Marlow called *Dr. Faustus.*

> FAUSTUS TO MEPHISTOPHILIS:
> *Tell me, what is that Lucifer, thy Lord?*

MEPHISTOPHILIS:
  Arch-regent and commander of all spirits.

FAUSTUS:
  Was not that Lucifer an angel once?

MEPHISTOPHILIS:
  Yes, Faustus, and most dearly loved by God.

FAUSTUS:
  How comes it, then, that he is prince of devils?

MEPHISTOPHILIS:
  O, by aspiring pride and insolence.
  For which God threw him from the face of heaven.

FAUSTUS:
  Where are you damned?

MEPHISTOPHILIS:
  In hell.

FAUSTUS:
  How comes it, then, that thou art out of hell?

MEPHISTOPHILIS:
  Why, this is hell, nor am I out of it.

By FEBRUARY OF MY first year in graduate school, I was in hell.

My birthday, February the thirteenth, had come and gone without joy.

By March I was nearly inert.

Since I had no alarm clock, I would wake myself by means of the radio. One station did not go on the air till six o'clock in the morning. Therefore I slept with the radio on, tuned to that particular station. I slept through its electronic crackles, then shot up when I heard "The Star-Spangled Banner."

The class I taught was scheduled for eight o'clock. I had enough time to shower and shave and go over my lecture notes, then walk to campus and acknowledge the freshmen when they entered the classroom.

But I was growing more and more oppressed under the dead weight of despair.

"De-spair" comes of the Latin word *desperari*. *Sperari* means "to hope." *De* cancels hope. To be without hope—to be hopeless—is not to believe in the goodness of tomorrow. Not even to believe in a tomorrow at all. It is to be stuck in the misery of today.

Several times I did not wake to "The Star-Spangled Banner." I slept till the news came on, then had to rush to class, arriving late, guilty and despising myself.

In medieval times people believed that hook-beaked devils sat on their chests while they lay abed, monsters that stared into their faces and pressed the breath from their lungs. Nor were these devils dreams. They were realities, the animal-bodies of melancholy. They terrified the people, for death and hell were coming right behind—tomorrow night, tomorrow night.

In order to be sure of waking, I took to sleeping on the uncomfortable floor with the radio close beside my head. But my paralysis was greater than my solutions.

I slept fitfully. I came awake before the radio woke me. But then the radio played and played, and I did not, I could not, get up.

Eight o'clock came and went.

I knew that my students sat waiting for me—till one by one they left the classroom and all the desks were empty.

This heaped guilt upon my devils. Guilt, too, is a heavy oppression. Guilt and desperation together were weights I could not throw off.

I tried to sing hymns:

What a friend we have in Jesus,
All our sins and griefs to bear . . .

Are we weak and heavy laden,
Cumbered with a load of care . . .

The effort only confirmed my wretchedness.

"FATHERS AND TEACHERS," SAYS Father Zosima, the wise monk in Dostoevsky's novel *The Brothers Karamazov*, "what is hell?"

The question is rhetorical. He answers it himself:

> *I maintain that it is the suffering of being unable to love. He who scorns his ability to love on earth, can go up to the Lord. But that is just his torment, to rise up to the Lord without ever having loved, to be brought close to those who have loved when he despised their love.*

> *People talk of hell fire in the material sense. I don't go into that mystery, and I shun it. But I think if there were a fire in the material sense, they would be glad of it, for, I imagine, that in material agony their still greater spiritual agony cannot be taken from then, for that suffering is not external, but within them.*

Zosima's thought falls near to mine.

If I choose to reject God's good-and-evil and replace it with my own sense of good-and-evil, then I have rejected his kingship and his domain as well.

God says that it is good—his good for me—that I obey his statutes and serve him in everything that I do.

I say that it is good—my good for me—to establish my statutes and serve my own desires. In other words,

I want to be king and lord of a kingdom myself. And since there is not room for two of us in the town, we must go our separate ways.

God may say, "Don't." Even for my sake (and this is his love): "Don't eat of the fruit of the tree of good and evil. For in the day you eat of it, you shall surely die."

It might be God's prerogative to make rules. But to me his rules are an unacceptable restriction of my freedoms.

I declare, "I want to be free!"

And the merciful God does not deny me my will, and I become the king of all over whom I have (an earthly) authority.

I command my wife and children, and they must obey. I lord it over my inferiors. I boss my laborers. I restrict *their* freedoms—but I do not love them as God loves them, and I make them serve myself.

And then comes the last day and the judgment.

But God had granted me my desire, and it is in my desires that I am resurrected.

That is: I still am king of my own kingdom.

But the torment is that I am also its only, solitary citizen.

I can see the everlasting love which God's children enjoy in heaven. But it is in contrast to that love that my self-serving love is proved to be my hell. My very being is my hell. I have chosen it, and I am forever an outcast.

As almost every other school in Edmonton, Canada, Concordia had a hockey rink. Hockey is to Canada what baseball is to the United States.

In spring the ice melted, and the rink became a wooden, oval wall surrounding dry land: a perfect field for football. We children of the neighborhood took it over.

But we played in socks. Therefore we looked for any stones the winter freeze had pushed up from the ground and threw them out of the rink.

I was probably the poorest player of the lot. Moreover, I threw, as they said, "like a girl."

So I would pitch my stones up toward the rink lights, always, always missing them.

It happened one day that my father caught me winging a rock at one of the pole-lights.

"Wally! Don't do that!"

"But I never hit anything."

"Those are six-thousand-watt light bulbs. More expensive than I have money to buy. You will not embarrass me!"

I have written before that my dad wore all black except for his clerical color. By the time he had become president of the institution, his eyebrows had lengthened. He twisted the ends of them up until they resembled a crow's wings flying. Dr. Wangerin's countenance could be very severe.

But I paid little attention to his injunction. Because I always missed.

Then I picked up a nice hefty rock, cocked my arm and let it go.

In the instant it left my hand, I knew. This one was frightfully accurate. Just below the light bulb the stone curved. It had reached the apogee of its flight. It just touched the bulb. The stone fell with a small shower of glass.

I stood stunned. So did the others, but they stood staring at me.

I said to them all, "Don't tell anyone."

I went to my brother Paul and commanded him blackly: "Don't tell dad! Especially don't tell dad!"

He didn't.

But when dad came into the bedroom to kiss us goodnight, his kiss burned on my forehead. He had an affectionate name for each of his children. Mine was "Ah-vee." Before leaving the bedroom he said, "Sleep tight, Ah-vee."

My stomach clutched. I was no longer his Ah-vee, but he didn't know that. He was kissing a boy who was a pretender, not his son. And the son hidden inside that boy suffered an unholy anguish.

After dad turned out the bedroom light, I pulled a book from under my covers and started to read by flashlight.

Mine was the upper bunk. Paul's was the lower.

He complained, not for the first time, that he couldn't go to sleep until I turned off the flashlight.

I refused. This time misery had drawn me taut.

Paul said, "Turn it off, Wally."

"Shut up."

"Wally, *please!*"

"Go to sleep."

In those days my brother showed his nervousness by laughing. He couldn't help it. But I hated his laughter because I thought he was mocking me.

Paul began to snicker.

"Quit!" I said. "Quit that!"

My outburst caused him to giggle.

"If you don't stop that, I have to hit you."

My threat broke all his restraint, and he laughed out loud. He sprayed spit between his tongue and his teeth.

So I climbed down from the top bunk and made a fist, protruding one sharp knuckle. I hit him on the bony part of his shoulder. He stopped laughing. He rolled himself into a ball and started to cry.

He said, "You don't care if nobody likes you."

That was worse than a hit. It was the truth.

Six

NEAR THE END OF MAY neither food nor study could sustain me. I had in anger given up writing poetry long ago. God had defeated me, but I couldn't work up the least tremor of anger. This is the way it was. This is the way it would ever be.

Each of my four classes required a paper before the end of the term. If I could hardly stir up my indigent soul, I could not write at all.

During my last year in college—this time in Fort Wayne, Indiana—my theology professor and his family befriended me. His wife had praised my poetry. She and I would talk late into the night drinking scotch. Their children delighted in my visits.

On the last Saturday of the month, I sped north seeking their friendship, hoping to be washed in friendship. Perhaps they could ease my sorrows and strengthen me for my final run at finishing my classes. Then there would only be the thesis left to write—and I had the summer to complete that.

But the professor and his wife were fighting in mute silence. The house was cold. That Saturday night I tossed about, unable to sleep. In the morning I drove away with scarcely a goodbye.

The whole world was in bloom. Wheat fields were green with tender shoots. In the towns, lawns were mowed and rose bushes were budding. Redbud trees beclouded the woods with sunrise colors. All this beauty grieved me. For nature obeyed the turning of her seasons while I lived in gloomy hell.

One thought occurred to me. Why couldn't I take incompletes in my classes in order to write my four papers during the summer. Surely I would rise and work when the pressures eased up.

Not glad, not hopeful, but with a little less trembling I arrived in Oxford. I busied myself and shut off my mind by cleaning my apartment, waiting for Monday morning.

And so it was that I knocked on Dr. Peterson's office door. He called me in and offered me a chair. He did not close the door to his secretary's room.

Dr. Peterson was a kind man, a fair man, short, olive-skinned, his head covered with coal-black hair. I don't think he ever raised his voice. Never. And I don't remember that he did not have time for those who knocked.

He asked what I wanted.

I explained my difficulty, then presented my proposal:

"Can I take incompletes in my classes and still retain my fellowship?"

Softly he said, "No. You can take the incompletes. And you can come back in the fall. But you will have to pay for the education yourself."

I started to cry.

Dr. Peterson did me the small favor of closing his door so that my sobs would not be heard outside his room. I appreciated the gesture. In a while my crying subsided.

Then he said, "What's the matter?"

What I said next surprised me. My tongue spoke what my mind had not expected.

I said, "I'm having trouble with God." Again Dr. Peterson sat with me as long as I wept. His eyes held an expression of genuine sympathy.

But no was no. Every possible window had been closed. I must remain in hell forever.

WHEN I WAS YOUNGER and at home, I don't think I spent more than three days suffering my private ostracism. Meals were especially painful. Each of the older boys had our own personal plates: Mine was as red as beets (for I like them). Paul's plate was as green as beans. Philip's was yellow. Mike's may have been blue. Or black.

My father concluded every meal by reading a devotion. And we prayed a prayer that Paul and I had learned from our grandfather Wangerin:

O give thanks unto the Lord
for he is good
and his mercy endures forever.

Customs like these kept tight the ties of our family. But customs rejected me. Wally was a liar.

When finally I could take it no longer, I determined to go to my father and confess my sin.

The walk from our house to Concordia's Administration Hall went through a stand of trees and across a broad lawn. As I took that walk, I thought of the spanking I would get. My butt tingled.

I pulled open the building's great door and entered.

Dad's office was down a dark hallway. On the doorframe he had affixed a small plate that read (white letters on a black background): "Dr. W. Wangerin, President."

I knocked as softly as a butterfly's kick.

But it was enough.

"Come in."

I went in.

Dad always arranged his office so that he sat behind

his desk when people came to talk with him. I might have taken a chair, but I didn't. I walked to that desk and pushed my stomach against it. He raised his eyebrows, and I spoke.

I told him the truth then bowed my head, awaiting my punishment. It was our mother who spanked us for disobedience. My father spanked us only once. He commanded Paul and me to go into his home study. Soon he entered the room. He snapped his belt from its pants-loops and folded it. This was, as we remember it, the belt we said had lights on it. Actually, they were small, cut reflectors of various colors.

Now, in his college office, I told him about the shattering of the six-thousand-watt light bulb and of all the lies I had been telling. Then I fell silent and bowed my head. I expected his first spanking to be followed now by a second, and this much harder than the first.

I heard him get up. His leather chair squeaked. I heard him come around the desk. I squeezed my eyes shut and saw nothing but pins of red.

Then I heard nothing else.

In a moment my father encircled me with his arms. Oh, Jesus, Jesus, how I bawled.

When my father drew back, he said, "Well, you'll have to pay for a new bulb."

So I LEFT DR. Peterson's office. I walked out into daylight utterly blank, not a thought of what I might do next. Simply, I kept walking.

High Street was Oxford's main street. It ran straight out of the town and into open country, where it became a graveled road. And I kept walking.

I may have walked several miles before I saw a flock of sheep cropping grass in a fenced field. A grove of trees bordered the back of the field. The trees were leafy, obscuring the view beyond.

Suddenly I was filled with rage toward the sheep. Whey-faced, dumb animals! Fat and passive, careless, weak, obedient!

I wanted to run at them, screaming until the whole flock was terrorized. I wanted to see them stumble and fall—woolen, spineless pillows! It would relieve me of my own heart's weaknesses.

But before I could, a farmer in overalls and a John Deere cap came through the leafy grove. He made a nickering sound in his throat.

Immediately the sheep turned. So did the farmer. And they all trooped through the trees and were gone, and I was once again left alone.

But the sight of the sheep had broken my soul.

I said, "I want to be a sheep."

As soon as I said it I realized that it had been a prayer and that I was praying to Jesus—the good Shepherd.

"I don't care any more. I want to be protected and led. I want you to make decisions for me."

Shortly before this I had read an article in *Time* magazine wherein a man was quoted as saying, "All Christians are sheep." The words were meant as a sneer. But now for me the words were hope. I could let everything go. Just everything, and be light again.

Seven

Once, when I was spending my first months at Concordia in Milwaukee, my father sought to heal my homesickness by suggesting that I read the Gospel of John. John, he said, could most persuade me of the love of God.

When I returned to my efficiency apartment that Monday, I remembered his suggestion.

I lay belly-down on my bed and let the book fall open and began to read the story in John's ninth chapter.

> *And as Jesus passed by, he saw a man which was blind from his birth.*

Jesus heals the blind man by spitting on the ground and making a clay of his spittle, with which he anoints the blind man's eyes.

When the man obeys Jesus' command to wash his

eyes in the pool of Siloam, he comes back seeing.

You might think that the miracle would cause praise and joy among his friends. Instead, his neighbors doubt that he is the same fellow who had sat begging by the gate.

"He is not like him."

But the blind man tries to affirm that indeed, "I am he." And he says, "A man that is called Jesus made clay and anointed mine eyes, and said unto me, Go to the pool of Siloam, and wash. I went and washed, and I received sight."

"Where is this man?" the neighbors ask.

And he answered, "I know not."

And then the story tells of the man's slow loss of his identity.

He is sent to the Pharisees, who also ask him to explain the change in him.

He simply repeats what he has already said to the neighbors.

They say, "He cannot be of God, because he keepeth not the sabbath day." They refuse to believe the blind man's tale, and so he is diminished because his truth is judged to be a lie.

Next the Pharisees haul his parents into court and demand that they tell the truth about their son.

But his parents are afraid of these leaders of the people. So both his mother and his father choose not to support their son. They tell the Pharisees, "By what means he was healed we know not. Nor do we know who healed him. He is of age. Ask him."

The Pharisees have already agreed that if anyone should confess that Jesus was the Messiah, that one should be put out of the synagogue.

Even so, the man is rejected by his family. That essential part of his identity is shorn away.

I am that man. I too lost essential pieces of myself, even my identity.

The leaders call the man born blind back into court.

"Give God the praise," they say to him. We say today: "Do you swear to tell the truth, the whole truth, so help you God?" Both phrases mean exactly the same thing. A witness is put under an oath.

The Pharisees say, "We know that this man is a sinner."

But the man born blind clings to the truth in spite of the consequences. He answers, "Whether he be a sinner or no, I know not. One thing I know, that whereas I was blind, now I see."

Truth gets him into greater trouble. Nevertheless, by a paradox, his spirit soars. In fact he grows down-right jolly. I suspect that the loss of his old identity is setting him free.

The Pharisees tell him to repeat the story of his healing.

He does, but then he asks, "Will ye also be his disciples?" See? Freedom makes him bold, even ironic— again, in spite of the consequences.

The Pharisees, the leaders of the people, now revile him. "Thou art his disciple." Behold! A new identity, though spoken by ignorant men. They continue, "We know that God spake unto Moses. As for this fellow, we know not whence he is."

The blind man is fearless. He is lighter and lighter on his feet. Such is the stripping of all that he was.

As I read this story in the Bible, I began to think of my own persistent loss of self. But here was a completely different outcome.

The man blind from birth answers and says to his judges, "Why, herein is a marvel!—that ye know not from whence he is, and yet he hath opened mine eyes. Now we know that God heareth not sinners. But if any man be a worshiper of God, and does his will, it is that one whom God heareth. If this man were not of God, he could do nothing."

"Thou wast born in sin," the Pharisees explode, "and dost thou teach *us?*"

Then the last part of his identity is torn away. The leaders of his people throw him out—out of the synagogue, out of his society, out of all by which he knew himself until that moment.

He is a nothing. But he is free.

When I finished the biblical story, I found myself once again at the fenced field full of sheep. A nothing.

But Jesus meets the man born blind (which means that he who lived in darkness is given light again). Jesus names himself, and the man falls down and worships him.

By this act alone is established a relationship between him and the Son of God. Christ raises him up with a fresh and everlasting identity. He is, as it were, born again.

That is what I prayed for. To be free. To be one sheep of the shepherd. To give over what tatters I had left to Christ.

Now then. In the days that followed I thought about identity. In fact, I had the freedom to consider the issue without fear of any bad consequence.

I thought about it this way:

So, I might fail all four classes. What did that mean? It meant no more than that failure did not *have* to be failure where I was concerned. Instead, it would merely determine the who that I would be.

Let's say that graduate school is a mountain. Then let's say that I am a river. The river flows to the mountain but cannot climb it. The student flows toward a master's degree but cannot finish it. So the river (and the student) simply flows around the mountain. What failure is there in that? It becomes the natural shape of the river. Draw a map, and there is the river, exactly as it ought to be: bending left unashamed, flowing as it ought to flow, down to the sea.

Likewise, if I cannot climb the mountain of a master's degree, that will be my shape and my identity hereafter. I shall have been shorn of my old identity. But if I hadn't been, how could I be resurrected as fresh and new? I will do something else, and *that* will be the me I best can know.

So I approached the four papers my classes required. And here was a wonder: since I didn't *have* to do well, since what should be would be, since, therefore, I was fearless, I found the writing to be no labor at all. In a week I had composed them and had turned them in.

And for each paper I received an A.

Nice, but not necessary.

And here was the best evidence of my freedom:

The last thing, the last test of that semester, was to be an oral examination before a panel of three professors. One of these was the man who had worked with me to come up with a topic for my master's thesis. I don't remember the second man. But the third was the fellow who had insulted his whole class by speaking of male and female parts in disgusting language—the same professor whom I had insulted by dropping his class.

Sometime during the examination he asked me a question regarding Coleridge's poem, "Kubla Kahn."

My answer did not please him. It was too flip, too careless.

I said, "Well, it's about a park and a river."
He folded his hands and icily quoted:

In Xanadu did Kubla Kahn
A stately pleasure-dome decree:
Where Alph, the sacred river, ran
Through caverns measureless to man
Down to a sunless sea.

Rivers and rivers—and like the man born blind, I was quite cheerful in spite of my foolish answer and his cold scorn. Such is freedom.

In the next year I received my master's degree.

The Second Part:
YE WATCHERS AND YE HOLY ONES

Eight

THANNE AND I WERE MARRIED in August on the 24th, 1968—St. Bartholomew's Day. In 1970 I began to teach at Evansville University in southern Indiana.

I taught freshmen in composition, as I had at Miami University. I also taught the history of the English language and a course in moral absolutes.

The university sat across Lincoln Street from the great stone edifice, Redeemer Lutheran Church.

We had one son and soon were to adopt a second son.

My office was in a complex of quonset huts, cramped, with a single chair to accommodate students, and an old wooden desk.

In those days I wrote short stories and one long play. And then a novel, *Wind Ward*, which was rejected by seven or eight publishing houses. I sent it to Harper

& Row, who also rejected it but encouraged me to keep on writing. Then I wrote a second novel, *The Book of the Dun Cow,* which Harper did accept.

We attended Redeemer Lutheran Church, which Dr. Grabill, chairman of the English department, called "that mausoleum across the street." David Wacker was its pastor.

David, a tall, strong-boned man with a horsey face, had played basketball in college and again at the seminary in St. Louis. He could leap beneath the basket, reach for the ball that had been looped behind him, then slam it home before he dropped down again—all in a single, fluid motion. When he entered the pulpit, David would yank his cincture up with two hands, the way an athlete does his belt, and then wipe the back of his hand across his lips: ready, set, preach!

He would regularly lope from Redeemer across the lawn to my office in order to discuss the lessons upon which he planned to preach the next Sunday. I saw him coming every time. I had more knowledge of theology than he. Thanne and I sat in a pew second from the front. He shouted. He scarcely needed a microphone. Often I would hear my illustrations in his mouth.

In 1973 he made a proposal. He thought I had a vocation.

"You should be in the ministry," he said.

"I'm teaching," I said.

"No, you should be preaching," he said.

"I want to give my life to writing."

Wacker wanted me to be his assistant while I finished my seminary education. Then I would be ordained and become a full-fledged pastor. My position at Redeemer would be elevated. I would become a pastor in dual ministry with him.

I didn't say no. Neither did I say yes. I wasn't sure that I *did* have a vocation. My brother-in-law once said, with no humor, with perfect sincerity, "God expects his pastors to be poor." As poor as a monk.

Wasn't I still studying for my doctorate in English literature? Besides, even from the third grade I thought of myself an author. I was a storyteller. That was flat. I had spun tales for my brother Paul in bed at night. And someone had donated typewriters to my elementary school on which I could pour forth stories as fast as my imagination flowed.

In the eighth grade I wrote a very short story and entered it in a school contest. The story, though it was fiction, had nonetheless been based on my family. The submission took first prize. With the prize came an opportunity to read it aloud before an all-school assembly.

After that presentation I noticed that my schoolmates and my teachers saw me in a new light. They talked to me with a kind of sympathy. Why? Well, they believed what I had written! My, my, my.

History class followed the assembly. The instructor was a little man with a bald head. When his students acted up, he would write out his entire lesson on the blackboard, commanding us likewise to write his words in our notebooks. Anger turned his bald head red.

This is what he did after the assembly. But I didn't obey him. I was lost in a new thought: if people believed my fiction, and if they were changed thereby, then I had changed the world ever so slightly. Oh, I thrilled in the power. More wonderfully, no one knew what I had done. I was a secret creator. Therefore, I could shift reality with impunity.

That summer I wrote my first novel.

Why should I give up writing for preaching? This was the reason I couldn't say yes to David's proposal.

DURING A DARK PERIOD of the Kingdom of Judah's history, Hilkiah the high priest discovered the Book of the Law (the core of Deuteronomy) buried in the Temple. He gave it to the secretary of King Josiah, a man named Shaphan. Shaphan then read it aloud to the king.

Here is the power of God's sacred word: to change the one who hears it.

"When the king heard the words of the Book of the Law, he rent his clothes. And the king commanded Hilkiah, saying, 'Go, inquire of the Lord for me, and for the people, and for all Judah, concerning the words of this book that has been found. For great is the wrath of the Lord that is kindled against us, because our fathers have not obeyed the words of this book.'"

That divine dialogue continues even down to today. God's word moves King Josiah. Josiah's plea is answered by God who spoke then through the prophetess named Huldah. Huldah said that God said, "Because your heart was penitent, and you have humbled yourself before the Lord when you heard how he spoke against this place, I have also heard you."

Even so does God breathe new life into his written word today, speaking again and again to people like me.

It was in the fall of 1973 that I returned to Miami University in Oxford, Ohio, in order to complete my class preparations for the PhD. Our third child had just been born, a girl. I left Thanne with the three children at home.

That summer President Nixon had been under fire. He resigned in August. Much of our telephone talk, Thanne's and mine, was about Richard Milhous Nixon. I often heard our children playing in the background. Thanne was doing yeoman's work.

September turned into a burning October. The bright candle of October was then blown out by grey November. Mine, too, was yeoman's work, but not nearly as hectic as Thanne's.

Now, a reading knowledge of two languages was required of every doctoral candidate. I chose German and Latin. I prepared for the German examination by reading and translating Günter Grass. For the Latin I began to translate the Gospels and Paul's epistles as written in Jerome's Vulgate Bible.

My pot-smoking Texan friend never returned to Miami after receiving his master's degree. Nor have I seen him since. What I remember most are the nights when he came to my apartment seeking some sort of consolation, and that my own impoverished faith could not sustain him. It might have been better to talk with him now, since my efforts were no longer rote but were spoken out of a genuine faith. I fear that his black depressions overcame him and that his heart wilted.

But the situation had been ministerial after all. However false my service, I'd been like a pastor counseling a person in need.

And that could be the vocation Wacker saw in me.

Günter Grass, the Vulgate Bible, a course in Romantic literature—I never did not think about my Rubicon. Should I teach and write? Should I be ordained?

Back at Miami I took up the midnight walks I'd walked six years earlier. Cold December forced me into a heavy coat. My ears froze, and I breathed steam into the air. But I felt no desperation. I kept noodling my call, whether I had one or not.

A light, merciful snow began to fall. Flakes caught on my coat. They alighted on my face and melted. Such precious attentions of the Father!

The Catholic Newman Center was always unlocked, day or night, inviting the weary in. On a table in its library there lay an enormous Vulgate Bible. One night after sundown I sat under the library's globe lights—the walls of the small room in shadow—and I found myself translating Paul's letter to the Romans, chapter eight.

I always wrote my translations on ruled paper in a binder.

So I was writing in English verse twelve and verse thirteen without much thought or attention. It was a slow, pedestrian business. Then the fourteenth verse presented itself to me.

I read, *Quicumque enim spiritu Dei aguntur, ii sunt filii Dei.*

Something caused me to breathe a little faster, almost to pant.

I wrote my translation: "For whoever is led by the spirit of God—"

Then I stopped. The verse engaged me. What *about* those who allow the spirit of God to lead them?

I wrote again the clear and simple answer:

"They are the sons of God."

Ah, dearest Jesus, that is what I wanted to be! I wanted to be a child of God. Then what did I have to do? I had to let God lead me. And in what pathways? God's, not mine. Mine was to teach. God's was to serve him. And how better to serve him than in ministry?

There it was. I knew how I would answer Wacker's proposal.

I closed the big Bible, walked through the cold back to my room, sat down, and wrote two letters

One was to David Wacker saying that I accepted his offer.

The other was to my wife, saying that I loved her dearly—and that our lives were about to take a radical turn.

Nine

BEFORE GOING HOME THAT CHRISTMAS, I had chosen a topic for the doctoral dissertation: medieval poetry, and specifically, the Pearl Poet.

I piled in my office the books I needed to study the Pearl Poet. But I said to myself that if I should go in another way, I would take all these books back to the library and never write a dissertation at all.

REDEEMER GAVE ME A small, windowless, cinderblocked room in which to do my work.

My work: I began immediately to teach an adult Bible class. I became the youth group's leader. I administered the entire educational program at church. As for Sunday School, I wrote up the lessons myself, selected the best teachers, asked them to meet with me weekly, whereat I gave them my lessons and walked the teachers through them, after which they were to fill them in as their own lesson plans for Sunday.

Both Wacker and I visited the sick. I preached once a month. I loved the people.

And, in free time, I wrote my second novel.

Wherever I went, I carried the developing manuscript in a briefcase, always ready to pull it out and write another page.

Since we lived on two acres, Thanne and I supported ourselves by planting a large vegetable garden. There was a strawberry patch. The property had come with a chicken coop, so we raised chickens for eggs and meat. My brother-in-law taught me how to chop off a chicken's head: lay the bird on a log, stroke its feathers until it grows a little woozy, then bring the machete down just behind its head. He taught me, too, how to butcher the chicken.

Our children called the chicken coop a "chicken poop." They stayed away from it because the roosters would run after them, pecking the backs of their knees. Thanne and I would sit together on a bench-swing in the evenings. We adopted our fourth child, and then we were six: Joseph, Matthew, Mary, and Talitha, their mother and their father.

Dave Wacker and I drove to Concordia Seminary in St. Louis. We had scheduled a meeting with the dean, Dr. John Damm, a stout, rosy man filled with good will. We asked him whether my work at Redeemer could count as my vicarage. Vicarage was a period of internship required of all seminarians.

Damm said yes. But then he folded his hands on the desk and told us sadly that we might run into some serious problems ahead.

A strongly conservative faction had arisen in the Lutheran Church with every intention of booting the "liberal theologians" out of the seminary. By the time I finished my vicarage, Damm said, he and the faculty could be gone.

We said we would take our chances. After all, I had received a call from the Lord.

One Sunday several African Americans attended Redeemer—black faces in a mob of white.

After services they asked to speak with David Wacker.

On Monday he told me what they wanted.

They were from another Lutheran parish, Grace, situated in the inner city. They had lost their last pastor. Before they called a new one, they thought it right to spend time investigating whether they should call another, or whether, as they said it, they should close their doors. On any given Sunday no more than twenty-five or thirty people came to worship.

Would someone at Redeemer serve them both to preach and to help them with their investigation?

Wacker was a genial fellow, ever hopeful. Right away he told them yes.

Now he wanted to know if I might add Grace to my other duties. I told him yes.

During my second year at Redeemer, the conservative element became virulent. A man named Pruess was president of the synod. When he took office he announced that he was determined to run Dr. John Tietjen, the president of the seminary, out of office. Preuss launched his crusade by bring charges of heresy against Tietjen. That process would take a while.

But alarming the general church members started right away.

The president of the Indiana district traveled to each church in his jurisdiction, decrying the heresies infiltrating Lutheranism. He was Woody Zimmerman, a man with a limp. Because Redeemer was one of the largest churches in his district, he visited us more than once. Moreover, Redeemer made wonderful offerings both to the church in Indiana and to the church at large.

Mournfully, Zimmerman blamed what he called "Gospel reductionism." The *right* doctrine, he said, divided the biblical principles of Law *and* Gospel. Now professors at the seminary were teaching that even the Law was given by God as Gospel. It was all under the tender mercy and the loving-kindness of the Lord.

For little Grace Church I worked up a questionnaire and carried it house to house. I wanted to sit in living rooms and talk with the families face to face.

Here is the gist of questionnaire:

Did Grace want to close its doors? Or did it believe it had a genuine mission from God to serve the inner city?

Could Grace grow large enough to support a pastor?

And if so, should that be pastor be black or white?

The results heartened me. Yes, they had a mission. People of the neighborhood were very poor. Many of them, though they considered themselves to be members of the Baptist church, never went to church at all. Even Baptists knew little of the Bible.

As for supporting a pastor, Grace might have had eyes bigger than their stomachs. They assured me that they could—if only everyone gave true tithes and emptied their purses for the sake of the Lord.

White or black? They had no nevermind as to that.

We set Sunday morning services at a late hour: 11:30 so that either Wacker or I could rush from Redeemer's ten o'clock and preach the same sermon at Grace. As time went on, we split the responsibilities: Sundays David preached at Redeemer, I preached at Grace.

And indeed, under our care Grace did begin to grow.

The children that Thanne and I had adopted were African American: Matthew dark-skinned, Talitha light.

One Sunday after services I noticed Mrs. Ada Chester holding Talitha at arm's length, peering into the baby's face.

When she saw me, Ada asked, "Is she one of us?"

Not one of "ours." "Us." What she meant was: Is the little girl black like us?

I said yes.

Then Ada clasped Talitha to her breast and fairly sang her happiness.

Over the Christmas holidays, 1975, someone slipped a letter under the doors of the offices of all the seminary faculty (all except five who were deemed righteous). The letter announced that they were fired. They had two weeks to clear out their offices. Those who lived in seminary houses were not given much more time to move out of their homes.

A large portion of the student body responded in a most dramatic way.

They gathered outside of the gym, then processed, each with a white cross, to the chapel doors. On the doors they remembered Martin Luther, who nailed his Ninety-Five Theses to the door of the castle church in Wittenberg. They too posted their own theses to the chapel doors.

They planted their white crosses on the lawn: one cross for every faculty member who had been so deleteriously removed. And then they walked out. It was a crucial decision. They knew not where to go.

So the faculty voted to support their students. Straightaway they set up another seminary, even before they had a building in which to teach: Concordia

Seminary in Exile, or Seminex. *They* would see their seminarians' graduation.

Bombast followed. Not only should the heretics be kicked out of office. They should be cut from the church roster of ordained preachers. They should leave the synod altogether.

After that I told Redeemer's church council that I intended to finish my own seminary training at Seminex, since the professors there had been my professors before.

There might be, I said, hell to pay.

The council accepted my plans kindly, without a murmur. Perhaps they could not see what I saw coming.

But tensions grew. Indeed, Lutherans were alarmed. And passions made enemies of brother and brother, sister and mother. The church was tearing apart.

David Wacker threw himself into the cause. The big man intended to fight for guys like me.

On the other hand, a very good fellow named Henry Loppnow came to Thanne and me, begging us in all sincerity (for he truly loved us) to change our plans. He taught our children at the Lutheran school. He had accompanied Thanne on evangelizing forays. His children were in my youth group. He admired my preaching.

But we saddened our dear Henry. We couldn't do what he hoped that we would do.

An off-shoot synod was formed by pastors who were sympathetic to the "liberals." (Remember? "Gospel reductionism.") In this little synod (which they named The Association of Evangelical Lutheran Churches, the AELC), students who graduated from Seminex could be ordained and thereafter find placement in one of its parishes.

Woody Zimmerman warned congregations like Redeemer that they held their properties at the synod's behest. If any one of them should leave the synod, they would lose their land and their church buildings. It was a velvet threat.

During the autumn of 1976, I drove back and forth between St. Louis and Evansville on Interstate 64. At Seminex I took my final classes. In Evansville I took care of the people of Grace.

The closer we came to Christmas and my graduation, the more agonized did the members of Redeemer become. As I had chosen Seminex, so I chose to be ordained in the AELC. One must follow the other.

And *if* I was ordained outside of the Lutheran synod, what should Redeemer do with me?

In January 1977 I was ordained. David Wacker preached for the ceremony. The church was jammed with friends and parishioners. We were all jubilant. And my face burned red with gladness and gratitude to God.

But no one spoke of a contract for my new service at Redeemer as a full-fledged pastor, working by Wacker's side.

If fact, there were no plans for such a contract. Nor would I ever be installed at Redeemer.

David Wacker faltered.

"I have to think of my church," he said.

Early that year I happed to look at the budget for 1977. I ran my finger down the list of expenses. I did not find the line item for an assistant minister.

I took the budget to David.

He said, "I'm sorry. I am very sorry. The council voted to close that position."

My face burned, but not for gladness.

I pointed out that it had been the *whole* congregation, in an official assembly, that had voted me in two years ago. Therefore it must be the whole assembly and not some committee that can vote me out.

He agreed. With what emotion I cannot recall.

So an official assembly was scheduled for a Sunday after worship.

As it happened on that particular Sunday, Grace's services were done earlier than usual.

I drove back to Redeemer and walked into the fellowship hall. I stood behind the assembled members. The meeting was still in session. I had thought it would have been over by now. The only reason I'd come back was to pick up my family and drive us all home.

Member after member got up and said something like, "We love Walt, but . . ."

In all that discussion, only one woman stood up and reminded the congregation that it had made a commitment to me.

"But that was before . . ."

Finally the congregation took a vote. Overwhelmingly, people rose up to be counted as against the matter at hand.

"No."

Before anyone else, Thanne saw me in the back and came to stand by me.

Then the rest of the people saw me too. Many of them walked out of the hall with their eyes down. A number were crying.

One woman with her husband approached Thanne and me sobbing so deeply that she couldn't speak. Her husband, apparently, had nothing to say.

When the woman found her voice, she said, "How can you do this to us?"

Ten

WHERE COULD I GO BUT to Grace? I don't remember how we fed ourselves in those days. I only remember Thanne's frugality.

She had grown up on a farm. Farmers' daughters learned how to stitch and sew, how to can vegetables, how to turn fruit into jam. We ate broccoli. And beets, though Matthew hated beets and refused to swallow them. I told him that he could not get up from the supper table until his beets were gone. He held them into his mouth until they had been sucked white. I suppose he got their benefit after all.

We clothed ourselves in hand-me-downs. Someone gave us second-hand bicycles. The books we read to the kids came from the library. Otherwise, I wrote stories for them—many of which I've published as picture books.

And Grace had decided: Yes, they would call a pastor.

Grace Church was founded in 1938. It was a mission congregation in those days. The man who founded it sought members from among the most educated people of the neighborhood. Teachers, mostly. He was a very good minister, and the church flourished. And because many of its members had graduated from college, they administered the congregation according to a high standard. The organist eschewed gospel songs. She played Bach. And since the choir sang from a stall divided from the chancel by a low wooden wall, neighbors said that they were "hincty." Proud. That the choir thought that they were angels.

So they began. But in the last two decades, their pastors served two parishes, one white and one black. One after the other, these men chose to live closest to the white church. They were white.

Mrs. Allouise Story was one of those women who had headstrong opinions and absolute convictions. She had graduated from the Tuskegee Institute for black students. She knew what was right and what was wrong.

She sat on Grace Church's call committee. One day she came to my office at Grace uncharacteristically smiling.

"I can't wait. I know that I should wait, but I can't."

Then she handed me a formal sheet of paper. The call committee had taken a vote and was asking me to come and be their pastor.

My FATHER HAD ALWAYS said that it was the Holy Spirit who told him whether such an invitation were a true call or not.

I never understood this. How did the Holy Spirit talk to him or move him in the right, the holiest, direction? Even after my ordination a call seemed just a contract, church to person. You sign contracts.

But the Holy Spirit was indeed in Grace's call—because they were a people calling me. I began to realize that for me it took a congregation of faithful *people* to make a call God's call and true.

I did not accept it right away. I cherished it, but Thanne and I had to discuss it first, and to pray. We talked with our children.

At the seminary I had lived in a large old house with a man from what was then known as Rhodesia in Africa. He was a short, powerful man, very black. He spoke English with a musical accent. His name was Farai Gambiza.

I invited Farai to spend a weekend with us in Evansville. I wanted to get his wisdom concerning vocations—especially one which would put a white man in a black congregation. And I asked him to preach on Sunday.

We spent Saturday in close conversation. He brought with him a wireless radio in order to keep up with the news from his country. It was very close to winning freedom, when the land would be named

"Zimbabwe." So he had thoughts and I had thoughts and we shared them together.

On Sunday he did preach. But it was another event during the service that caused him his deepest emotion—and mine too.

Mrs. Allouise Story got up to sing. She sang "Nobody Knows the Trouble I've Seen" in a thrumming alto. She sang unaccompanied. It was her voice alone, and the congregation hushed to hear it.

The longer she sang, the lower went Farai's head. We were sitting side by side in the chancel. Soon he began to shake his head. Then he said, "Nobody, nobody should sing like that." Allouise's singing was much too sorrowful for his soul.

His reaction caused the same reaction in me. My chest heaved and I fought not to sob. How would I lead the service if I did?

Afterward I put Farai's unspoken question to Allouise. "How can you sing so lowly?"

She straightened her back and humphed, "That's the way we were taught to sing at the Tuskegee Institute."

MRS. STORY DID THANNE and me a favor greater than we could have recognized in New Orleans.

In order for me to understand the position of black clergy and black congregations in the synod, she paid for our flights from Evansville to New Orleans. There was to be a convocation of African American Lutherans there.

Several hundred people attended, a sprinkling of white pastors in a black sea. Those who preached preached powerfully.

Mrs. Story had once said to me, "We shall have no 'tonin' at Grace Lutheran."

"'Tonin'" was a foreshortened version of "intoning." The word appears in the introduction to James Weldon Johnson's, *God's Trombones.* I'll quote the passage:

> *The old-time Negro preacher of parts was above all an orator, and in good measure an actor. He knew the secret of oratory, that at bottom it is a progression of rhythmic words more than anything else. Indeed, I have witnessed congregations moved to ecstasy by the rhythmic intoning of sheer incoherencies. He was a master of all the modes of eloquence. He often possessed a voice that was a marvelous instrument, a voice he could modulate from a sepulchral whisper to a crashing thunderclap. His discourse was generally kept at a high pitch of fervency, but occasionally he dropped into colloquialisms and, less often, into humor. He preached a personal and anthropomorphic God, a sure-enough heaven and a red-hot hell. His imagination was*

> *bold and unfettered. He had the power to sweep*
> *his hearers before him; and so himself was often*
> *swept away. At such times his language was not*
> *prose but poetry.*

Those "incoherencies" might be a series of "hu hu hu."

This is how the preachers preached in New Orleans, but with a vast intelligence, no "hu-hus." Fierce theology. And the people responded in dialogue: "Preach it, brother!" "Yes!" and "Ay-*men!*" And clap—oh, how they clapped. On the other hand, no one "fell out." That is, they didn't jump up and shout, or throw back their heads and swoon. These black Lutherans left such demonstrations to the Baptists and the Holiness churches.

I could never preach that way. But I didn't have to. "No 'tonin'," Mrs. Story had instructed me.

But I was moved. And I dearly wanted Grace to be a part of this African American society.

Therefore I found one of the leaders of the group and told him that Grace in Evansville might have to leave the synod. "If it did," I asked, "could we still join you?"

The leader said, "No. We already have enough walls to break down. That is one we do not need."

Once more I considered the invitation of the call committee, whether I should or should not become pastor of Grace. Hadn't Woody Zimmerman threatened with expulsion those congregations who didn't get with the conservative program? I was ordained not by synodical officials, but by an official of the breakaway church, the AELC.

If I accepted the call, Grace Lutheran Church might also be expelled.

Mrs. Story's second favor was one she didn't intend. She didn't even notice what she was doing.

On our first evening in New Orleans she took Thanne and me out for dinner. The restaurant was in cafeteria style, so we each could select food we liked. Once we'd sat down at a table, a waiter came to ask what drinks we wanted. I suppose this was a way that waiters could be tipped.

Now, our particular waiter, who was white, put his question to me. Mrs. Story indicated that she was the one paying. He should speak to her, not me. But the poor fool ignored the woman altogether, didn't so much as look at her. He did, however, put his question also to Thanne.

At that point Mrs. Allouise Story rose up like Sinai. Though she wasn't as tall as the young man, he seemed to shrivel down to size.

In my heart I said, "Overreacting, overreacting," meaning Mrs. Story.

This was my first lesson. Not only had I not seen the racism in the waiter's manner, but I didn't recognize the racism in me.

In time my mind was changed. This is what changed it: that one needs to *love* those who suffer oppression in order to know the signs of oppression himself, and actually to feel the oppression as his own.

IN SPITE OF EVERYTHING, Thanne and I said to Grace, "Yes."

We accepted the call.

Eleven

ONE OF THE MEMBERS OF Redeemer Church was a woman ninety years old. She could barely see. She was shaky on her walking stick and hunched down to tiny when sitting in a pew. Her daughter, exactly the age of my father, would lead her mother into church, the older woman leaning on the younger woman's arm: Mrs. Clara Scheiber and Ruth Scheiber, who was herself fifty-six.

Somehow Clara knew that I wrote short stories.

I received by mail an invitation on pasteboard, signed with a flourish, "Clara Schreiber." She asked if I would be so kind as to attend her for lunch in her home.

Ruth met me at the door of a small, green-shuttered bungalow.

Mrs. Schreiber herself was sitting behind a small table in their kitchen. I sat down across from her where cutlery and a dish were set.

Before we talked, Ruth fed me: roast beef, potatoes, corn.

Mrs. Scheiber said, "Ruth is my amanuensis. She has sight. She writes my words. You," she said, "are an author." At that time I was still unpublished, but she named my dream as if it were already true.

She said, "I have invited you here for three particular reasons."

Her first reason was that she wanted to renew old acquaintances.

"I knew your grandfather when he was pastor of our parish in Illinois. Fifty years ago and more. Mr. Schreiber was my husband. He was the principal of our Lutheran day school. Your father was but a boy. He and my Ruth sat in the same class."

Her second reason: "I have published a small book. I am an author like you."

A published author! I had never been in the company of a published author before. It caused my heart to trip faster.

She said, "If you wish it, I offer myself as your mentor. We will read our material one to the other and discuss the success or the failure of the composition. Perhaps I can be your Virgil to my Dante."

Her third reason made no sense to me.

She leaned over the table and spoke in an urgent whisper. "You should never have to dance in the dark."

Well, I was delighted to find a mentor in her.

Before I left, Mrs. Scheiber gave me a little home-work—not her own little book, but a biography of Chopin.

As we met week after week, I began to learn her story until I understood her enigmatic phrase "dance in the dark."

In the 1920s, during the days of Clara's young womanhood, German Lutherans lived by strict codes. Women were to be silent servers in the church. They couldn't teach men. They wouldn't be elected to church councils. Certainly they could not play roles in worship. They were to be members of the Ladies Aid and the Altar Guild, mothers, the cooks for church smorgas-bords. They could teach children. That sort of thing.

Outside of church they might write letters and postcards and hymns, if they were able. But any other writing—writing, say, a book—was considered vain-glorious, a vanity to be censured.

Nevertheless, Mrs. Schreiber wrote.

She had chosen to write a biography of Martin Luther's wife, Katherine.

She wrote longhand, of course, with an ink pen at the dining room table. But she waited until Principal Schreiber and the children had left for school, after she had finished her housework. Before her family came home she had put her pages and her books away. The project must be done in secret. Clara wrote and revised and typed the whole from September into the spring.

When her manuscript was completed, she returned it to the typewriting paper box and sent it to the single Lutheran publishing house.

She waited through the summer, though with little expectation that the publisher would publish a woman's work.

In September a thin envelope arrived by mail— from the publishing house. Once again Clara waited until she had the house to herself. By a wonderful Teutonic discipline, she washed clothes and ironed her husband's shirts.

Then she sat down at the dining room table.

Clara Schreiber slit the fold of the envelope with a paring knife, slipped out its single page, and read the letter.

"We will be pleased to put your book between covers. Congratulations."

"I was so ecstatic," she said to me, "that I held my hands on the top of my head, or it would just explode. I laughed and I twirled around the room like a child. And I danced. But before I danced I pulled the curtains closed. You should never have to dance in the dark like me."

Now, I tell you that story in order to tell you this.

On the Sunday of my installation as the pastor of Grace Church, after most of the people had left the building, I saw Mrs. Clara Schreiber sitting with her daughter in the last pew.

I walked to her.

She said, "But you will never leave the Lutheran Church, will you?"

It was perhaps a half-year after my installation that David Wacker took a call to Little Rock, Arkansas, and left Evansville for good.

In time Redeemer Church found another man to take Wacker's place. This man's installation, like mine, was to take place on a Sunday afternoon in a full and glorious worship service with Holy Communion.

I decided not to go. But Thanne planned otherwise. We had many friends at Redeemer. Friendship had not passed away with our leaving.

As a caution, she called the president of the congregation and asked whether she would be served with everyone else the bread and wine of the body and blood of our Lord Jesus.

The synod practiced—and still practices—the doctrine of "closed communion." That is, those who are not members of the synod will not be allowed to commune with them at their table. Ask me why and I will refer you to the synod's own theologians. I can't understand their reasons.

When I came home to our two acres, I found Thanne sitting under three trees on a knoll of our property. She was crying. Redeemer's president had dashed her hopes.

Oh, my poor wife! Locked out of the church where she had worshipped for seven years. Excluded from the ceremony her friends would attend.

But her tears were not for sorrow.

The next day she told me that they were for joy, because the act had set her free.

WOODY ZIMMERMAN WASN'T DONE with me yet. He wrote, and kept writing, letters to Grace Church, encouraging them to encourage me to colloquize. This was a way that I might be received again as a rostered member of the synod's clergy. Either I would take several classes at the seminary ("You and Your Synod") or I could submit to an examination. If three administrators of the synod found my doctrine to be sound, then I would be accepted again as a cleric in good standing.

For the sake of my congregation (they *ought* to be members of the Black Convocation) I chose the latter course.

So I drove once again to St. Louis, praying neither to be too arrogant nor to be too meek, but rather to state the facts and my beliefs clearly and in the baldest of terms.

My examiners were Preus, the vice president of the synod; Bohlmann, the president of Concordia Seminary; and Webber, an official on the Board of Education.

The "colloquy" shouldn't last more than an hour.

So we sat down in Bohlmann's office. And the examination went swimmingly. I answered every one of their questions in the affirmative. At the end of the hour, Preus leaned back, ready to pronounce, I am sure, their acceptance of me and my theology.

I said, "But you haven't asked me any questions about my theology."

Preus said, "Well, Woody Zimmerman told us that you were fine on that aspect. But okay. Here's my question . . ."

He knew that I had taken a course in the Gospel of John under a Seminex professor. He said, "If you don't agree with that professor's interpretation of John chapter six, I would say that you do indeed believe in the right doctrines."

The problem with John six was that my professor taught that that chapter had been inserted after the Gospel had been written. The synod taught that such an insertion denied the authorship of John.

I said, "He didn't touch on that topic."

Again, things seemed set for my acceptance.

But I could not help but tell him that I *did* believe something similar: that the Pentateuch, the first five books of the Bible, were not written by a single writer but were the combining of at least three different strands of the story.

And that was that.

Preus said, "Everyone is watching us so see whether we are obeying the law these days. I'm afraid you don't qualify."

His answer delighted me. There was no longer any doubt about my future.

Thanne, too, was relieved.

But Woody Zimmerman still urged the church not to leave the synod.

I simply posted his letters so that all the members could read them.

They were patronizing, not to say racist.

"Your synod has loved you and has taken care of you all these years." But Grace owned its own property. Woody's threat about leaving the synod had no teeth. Moreover, the synod had ignored Grace "all these years." The congregation had taken care of itself. And whenever an African American happened to visit a white church, pastors said, "We think that you would be more comfortable among your own kind. There is this black parish downtown . . ."

"Let me, please," Woody wrote, "continue to be your caretaker."

Soon Grace said to me, "How can we stop these letters?" Each one was an insult.

"We can leave the synod," I said.

In order not to be rash, I visited every family, asking for their preference. Every member said we should leave—except for two men. Both of them enjoyed synodical assemblies. And one had a position on one of its committees.

In the end they both agreed, if slowly.

Grace Lutheran Church said goodbye to the synod.

ONE SUNDAY, WHEN THE congregation was still filing up the aisle and kneeling at the rail for Holy Communion, we ran out of hymns to sing.

Into the silence the members began to hum in their soft, African voices. They hummed "Amazing Grace" and soon were enriching the hymn by harmonizing.

Amazing grace, indeed. Amazing was Grace Church.

My heart grew warm.

We, Thanne and I and our four children, were home.

The Third Part:
SUPERNAL ANTHEMS ECHOING

Twelve

GRACE LUTHERAN CHURCH—THE BUILDING itself—sat on a slight rise at the corners of Eliot (north and south) and Gum Streets (east and west). It was red brick. Beside it was a parsonage too small for my family.

The church's interior had essentially two rooms: the sanctuary upstairs and a fellowship hall down. Entering the church brought us to a small landing. On the left, stairs went up to the sanctuary. On the right, stairs went down to the basement hall. There were exactly twenty pews. Stand in the chancel and you can count eleven on the left and nine on the right: nine to leave room to walk in and up a single aisle. Each pew could seat six adults.

Stained glass windows darkened the room. The window over the altar depicted Jesus praying in Gethsemane, kneeling at a great rock, his elbows on the rock, his hands folded, his face looking up to heaven. From his face a radiance ascended. He was dressed as I had thought he would be dressed when I was a child seeking him, in a robe and sandals, his flesh a chestnut color.

There was no air conditioning.

To the left of the chancel was a small room in which the organ sat. To the right was my office, a tiny room with space enough for one desk and one straight chair. I nailed bookshelves to the wall. The only window was that of a door which opened to a metal fire escape.

My white presence in the neighborhood made its black pastors suspicious. They thought I planned to pillage their churches of members. Moreover, they assumed that some large synod was supporting us with oodles of dollars. In time they changed their minds, and though I wasn't invited to their gatherings, we came to a wary peace.

One evening while I was walking outside on Eliot, a woman came up to me.

"Watcha want, blue eyes," she said.

I said, "I'm the pastor of this church."

"Oops," she said and hurried away.

Here I was, in the inner city, where ladies of the night do roam.

The houses on Gum were shotgun houses: three rooms in a dead straight row. They had been built during the second world war and never torn down.

Impoverished folks dwelt in them. "Shotgun houses" because you could shoot through the front door and hit somebody in the back yard. At least that was the story. What did I know?

I knew this, that the inner city scared me. If anyone had asked me before I began working at Grace, "What kind of parish do you want?" I'd never have picked one in a neighborhood like this.

Late one night I was sitting in my office when a black man's face appeared at the window. I nearly yiped out loud, and tingling spread all up and down my spine.

Herman Thomas Sr. had warned me always to keep the doors locked.

This man turned out to be the husband of Cheryl Lawrence, a member of mine. He wanted to check me out, I'm sure. Also, he brought me a copy of a letter he was mimeographing. It announced that come the summer, inner city African Americans planned to throw up barricades on Lincoln Avenue. Lincoln was the street that people drove when they wanted to get from the better neighborhood east of us to the business section of Evansville.

We got along well enough, he and I. Philip Lawrence: he was impressed that I had chosen to make my office at Grace rather than somewhere else and that I had the temerity to still be here after the sun went down.

"Watcha want, blue eyes?"

It was precisely because I was scared that I determined to walk wherever I went—and to greet people who sat on their porches in the evening, rocking, fanning themselves, and sipping cool drinks.

"Hello."

"Mm-hmm," through a cavernous nose.

"I'm Walt Wangerin. I preach at Grace Church."

"Mm-hmm."

"It's a fine evening, isn't it?"

"Was the Lord that made it so, Reverent."

"Of course, of course."

"Praise the Lord."

"Yes, indeed."

A long, rocking silence, my interlocutor looking off. Finally, "Well, goodbye. I'll be seeing you."

"Mm-hmm."

I SMOKED A PIPE in those days. One morning I was sitting on the concrete steps in front of the church, smoking my pipe, enjoying the sun, and reading a novel.

A low-slung car drove past me down Eliot, made a slow right turn onto Gum, then suddenly slammed to a stop. The man inside leaned through his window and said, "What you doin' here?"

It took me a moment to realize that he was addressing me.

"Sitting. Reading. It's a beautiful day."

The man opened the car door and strode in my direction, looking everywhere but at me.

He wore a T-shirt with the sleeves cut off. The logo on the shirt read: "Semper Fi." His arms were as thick as my thighs. Though his cheeks were round, his Africa-black forehead could pound nails.

"That ain't no answer," he said. Now he stood over me, looking directly into my eyes, the sun shone something like a glory behind his head. "I axed you, motherf—, what you think you doin' on my streets?"

I said, "Reading, sit—" and closed my mouth. I should not be flip with this huge, military fellow.

I pointed behind me. More sincerely I said, "I'm the pastor here."

"Bull—"

"No. It's the truth. I preach here."

He said, "I been talkin' wif my woman, see. She in the house down there, painted red. She tol' me some mother stole her TV set."

"I'm a pastor. I would never steal anything."

"Com' yere," he said, turning and walking back to his car. "Come *here!*"

I followed him. He swung open the driver's side door.

"Look down there," he commanded me.

I did as he said, then sucked air. Lying on the floorboards was an enormous gun.

"That there," he said. "She's mah 'Menace.'"

He had named his gun. Apparently he loved weapons. "Menace" was a most appropriate name.

"Ah'm warnin' you, honkey. I been in the Marines. I'm sayin' you stole my woman's TV set."

"No," I protested. I think I must have been whining. "No, I didn't."

"You don' tell me the truf, Ah'ma twist you till you talk."

"I don't know what else to say. This *is* the truth. I never met your girl. I don't even know who lives in that house."

"Ohhh, you in trouble now."

Just then a convertible came driving down Gum Street. That car slowed too. In it sat the grown daughter of Gloria Ferguson, who was another member of Grace. She stopped beside the two of us. She said, "Pastor, I wanna see you when you got the time for me."

Then she drove off.

"Hoo-wee!" said the marine. "Hoo-wee! You don't know how close you come."

"Close" wasn't the word for it. "Terrorized." That was the word.

The man stuck his head into his car and reached to the back seat. Then he brought out a black case. He then popped the latches. The case contained a silver flute.

He said, "Man, Ah been carryin' this here flute, see, from Dixie to dawn. Tell you what. You loan me a fifty an' Ah'll leave this wif you till I come an' pay you back."

I didn't think twice about his deal. I went for my wallet.

"Well," I said, "I don't have anything more than a ten and a twenty. Would this be enough?"

It was enough.

He and his Menace and my thirty dollars drove away.

The man never came back for the flute.

A WOMAN FROM REDEEMER once came to Grace's church building. She knocked on the door of my little office.

"I came," she said, "to say that you are truly humble, Walt. Because you sacrificed a good life to come down here and serve these people."

Her praise was delusional, not to say racist. To come "down" to serve blacks in the inner city was no sacrifice at all. It was my elevation.

CHERYL AND PHIL LAWRENCE had three little children about the ages of our children. Her mother was named Mary Moore. Mary was a hard-working woman, patient and devout.

Mary's mother was a chipper little soul named Stella Mayes. Actually, Stella's real name was Australia, because *her* mother, Mary Moore's grandmother, had named her daughters after the continents, and when she ran out of continents she started on the states: Connet was for Connecticut.

Mary was a little girl when Grace Church was born, obedient then, obedient still.

At Christmas she sang the spiritual "Mary Had a Baby, My Lord." She dragged the song as though it were a mop and she a weary woman. "She named the baby Jesus, my Lord. She named the baby Jesus, my Lord."

I could not help but think of the Virgin Mary whose son she watched as he suffered the horrors of the cross.

Oh, Mary, don't mourn. It will all be well.

But it had not always been well with her family.

Before she died, Mary's grandmother had worked as a maid, cleaning rooms in a hotel on the Ohio River's waterfront.

She kept her money in a pouch that hung on a string between her breasts, underneath her shirt.

One day while she was sitting in her living room a young, skinny man opened her door uninvited. She knew the man and he knew her. He had a serrated kitchen knife.

He pointed at her shirt and said, "I want that-ere money you hidin', woman."

Mary's grandmother said, "Get outta my house."

The skinny man's hand shook. He seemed hopped up on some sort of drug. He said, "I'ma goin' stab you. Give me the money."

"Go on. Walk your skinny self outta my house."

The man reached under her shirt.

She bellowed, and he stabbed her under her left shoulder.

The point of the knife stuck in a rib bone and snapped off.

He yanked at the pouch, broke the string, took the pouch, and ran.

Mary Moore's grandmother took off the shirt. She washed the blood from her cut. She pulled the skin together and closed it with a butterfly bandage. The wound healed, leaving a pale scar on her brown chest.

Hers was a simple life. She lived by herself. This was in the 1940s. Mary was about seventeen years old. She would watch her grandmother daily sweep out the house and the front sidewalk too. The woman's backyard grew no grass. But she would sweep its hard dirt until it was clean enough to satisfy her standards.

Because she drew a down-low salary, she spent but pennies for food. She bought hog intestines. She'd clean them with salt and boil them the day long until they were chitterlings. Chittlin's.

A year later the woman began to feel a dull ache high in her chest. It went from bad to worse, and worst was that she could no longer make beds in the hotel. She coughed blood. Finally the woman became bedfast.

Her children took her to the doctor.

The doctor X-rayed her chest and found that the knife-point had broken from the rib bone and was traveling through her lung. Every time she took a breath the metal moved another millimeter deeper. It was too late for surgery.

To Mary's sorrow, her grandmother died.

Though white people were buried in the greater part of Oak Hill cemetery, they had set aside a section for African Americans only. At the interment, just as the Baptist minister was throwing clots of earth on the casket, one of Mary's aunts whooped and hollered and fell to her knees beside the grave.

ONCE WHILE SHE WAS visiting cousins in St. Louis, Mary went with them to their Holiness church.

When she came back home, she confided to me that the shouting and the dancing had thrilled her, though she had been baptized a Lutheran and would always be.

She whispered her words so that no one else should hear them.

Thirteen

BY THE GRACE OF GOD and through no doing of my own, I grew beautiful feet.

I knelt and prayed at the chancel rail in the early morning when no one else was present. I studied. I read the lessons for Sunday worship in Greek, the better to understand every word (God bless, after all, the education I received at Concordia). I preached, and people came.

We worshipped with thirty and then with forty. Many of these were not Lutherans or members of Grace Church.

I counseled those in trouble. Since this was not the regular practice of other ministers in the neighborhood, their people—as well as the unchurched—sat with me in my office. I learned a helpful device: to turn my attentions to my pipe, stuffing the bowl with tobacco when a person needed time and quiet to marshal her unhappy thoughts.

I, too, had suffered their sufferings. I had experienced despair in graduate school when God seemed absent. The *Deus abscondicus*. And after the grief, I had experienced the joy of finding Jesus again. I could, therefore, walk with a counselee through the dark night of his soul and into the sunlight.

After every service, I stood outside the church doors to shake hands and learn their names. If someone looked downcast, I offered to visit her.

One woman said to me, "I don't give flowers to the dead. What good does that do? I give them to the living." Then she said, "You preach beautifully."

Everyone who calls upon the name of the Lord shall be saved.

But how are they to call on one in whom they have not believed? And how are they to believe in one of whom they have never heard? And how shall they hear without someone to proclaim him? And how are they to proclaim him unless they are sent? As it is written, "How beautiful are the feet of those who bring good news!"

BY THE FOURTH YEAR of my ministry at Grace, we had established a joyful custom. On the Sunday evening before the week of Christmas, we gathered outside the church, bundled and hatted and happy. Then we went through the sharp December darkness to sing carols. Down the streets of the neighborhood we walked in a group, children bounding forward, adults striding behind, chattering, making congenial noises, puffing ghosts of breath beneath the street lamps.

Will it snow? It was cold enough to snow, and the air was still, and the stars salted the black sky like the hosts of heaven.

We stopped at the front porches of the old and the housebound.

The children clattered onto the porch squealing excitement because they thought we were about to surprise Miz Lillian Lander by suddenly appearing, singing. They pressed their faces against her window and roared, "Hark! The herald angels sing, glory to the newborn king—"

Miz Landers pulled back her window curtains. She sat and peered out and smiled.

"Jingle bells, jingle bells," we sang, folks shaking their key rings to the rhythm.

Our white children's faces were pinched pink, the black faces dusted with frost.

Finally—and this at every house—we sang, "We wish you a merry Christmas," and walked on.

After a carol or two for Miz Hattie Garner, she asked us to sing "Silent Night."

These children were no ordinary children. They were a choir. We called them "The Grace Notes." Brenda Dixon directed the choir on Sunday mornings. I had thought that rambunctious children should sit in the back of the sanctuary. Brenda said, "Absolutely not!" She wanted them up front where the congregation could see them and honor them. Up front, therefore, they sat.

"Silent Night." The carol softened the singing. On the third verse the child Dee Dee Lawrence began to sing a descant. Her voice soared high and high above us all so wondrously that it could break your heart. Miz Garner bowed her head. Parents began to cry. Dee Dee Lawrence flew up to the stars themselves and touched to the crystal sphere of heaven, and all the round sky rang.

This girl was eight years old with milk-chocolate cheeks and an oriental cast to her eyes. She blinked her eyes rapidly when she sang.

Our last stop was in St. Mary's Hospital where several members lay sick in bed.

There we divided into three bands of carolers. I led the third band into Odessa Williams' room. Thanne, Dee Dee, our children; several older youth, Herman Thomas Jr., coffee-brown, and Mary Moore's son Timmy, whose voice and whose person were an easy chair; and others trooped into the room with me.

I should have warned them of Miz Williams' condition, because the children's eyes grew wide when they saw her. They circled her bed but stood a foot back from it. They did not so much as touch the sheet, nor bump against the ledge of the dark window behind them.

They smelled corruption in the air. The skin of the sick woman's face, as dry as parchment, had been pulled too taut. Her cheeks were scooped hollows. The legs under her sheet were broomsticks—skinny her arms and fingers like pencils.

Dee Dee stood at the foot of Odessa's bed. My Mary stood across the bed from me.

"Sing," I whispered to the children, but they only shuffled their feet.

"What's the matter? Cat got your tongues?"

Mary said, "I think she can't hear us."

"Sing anyway. Unconscious people can hear."

As LONG AS I'D been at Grace, Odessa Williams was housebound. I carried communion to her small apartment, where I read Psalms and prayed. That is, I prayed when she permitted me to do my pastoral duty.

Odessa was a strapping, tall woman. She would pace while I visited, jabbing the air with the hand that held her cigarette, smoke-clouds whirling over her head. She walked in slippers crushed at the heels. The woman knew her mind. Volubly she poured forth her mind's store.

If the woman was upset with some infraction of mine, she kept her dentures in her mouth in order to hiss her *s*'s and to tick her *t*'s and clack the teeth together. But when she was in a softer mood, she left her dentures in a glass of water.

Miz Williams was especially watchful for her "chirren." Though she'd never actually heard them sing, she swelled with a grand, maternal love for them.

Generally, my infractions had something to do with her babies.

"You let 'em sit up front, y'hear?" How did she know about seating arrangements? How did she know what I, as a pastor, ought to be doing, and what I ought not?

I told her that, indeed, her "chirren" were placed in the "up-frontest" pews.

I failed to persuade the woman not to smoke.

She developed cancer.

She was moved first into St. Mary's nursing home and then onto the ward to live out the last days of her life.

WELL, SO MY GRACE Notes obeyed me. Wide-eyed, encircling Miz Williams, they sang a pitiful "Away in the Manger."

By the time the cattle were lowing, the very sounds of their voices comforted them, and the carol swelled.

And Odessa opened her eyes. Without moving the rest of her body, she twitched her eyes left and right, focusing on one child and the next.

Louder now, they harked it with the herald angels. Her "chirren" found in their chests the first noel that other angels sang.

Odessa began to frown, to frown and to nod, her eyes squeezed shut. "Mm-mmm!" And she chewed as if on a delicious piece of meat, the signs of the woman's fierce pleasure.

Odessa did not have her dentures in.

The next thing she did caused the children to grin and to laugh through their carol.

Odessa Williams raised her frail arms and began to direct.

She swept those arms and swooped them like batons.

And when their final carol came to an end, I said, "Dee Dee. 'Silent Night.'"

Cherubim entered my children—Odessa's children—and they sang.

And Dee Dee began her descant already on the first verse.

Odessa shivered visibly. Wildly she looked around until she found the blinking child. Then, again, she raised her arms and directed Dee Dee with a marvelous fervor. By long strokes she lifted Dee Dee from the ground. She pointed the way. The child trusted the old, old woman. So high did Dee Dee soar, so long did she hold the notes, that the room—the whole hospital!—became a chime of glass.

"Round yon virgin, mother and child."

Stroke for stroke with imperious arms, Odessa sent her on a flight to glory. Dee Dee's soprano ascended on a fountain of light. She was not a child anymore. She was the North Star.

"Jesus, Lord, at thy birth—"

And then Odessa brought her down by meek degrees to earth again, back into the room and to the foot of her bed.

"Jesus, Lord, at thy birth."

Then all the children stood in formation, perfectly still, smiling in silence and waiting. How could *anyone* move after such a wonder?

Well, I might have. The caroling was done. Odessa was tired. It was time to go home.

But the children expected more. And Miz Williams did not disappoint them. In a low, smoky voice, she began to preach.

"Oh, chirren," she said, "you my choir. Oh, choir, you my chirren too. Ain' no one stand in front o' you for goodness, no. You the bes', babies. You the for-sure best."

The children gazed at her and nodded. They believed her completely. My daughter's eyes glistened.

She too believed in Miz Williams, body and soul.

"Listen me," Odessa said. "When you singin', wherever you go for singin' Jesus, look on down to the front row. Whatchoo gonna see? They's alluz a empty spot. Know what's in that spot?"

The children shook their heads, but they knew that they *would* know.

"It's me," Odessa whispered. "'Cause I alluz been wif you. An' I'm a-gonna be wif you after my days and all my troubles is over. An' you know how I can say such a mackulous thing?"

The children didn't know. So she told them.

"'Cause we be in Jesus," Odessa whispered the mystery. She lifted up one long arm. "Babies, babies, we be in the hand o' Jesus, old ones, little ones, an' us an' you. Jesus got us in his hand, and ain' no one gonna snatch us out. Jesus, he don' never let one of us go. Never. Not never."

So said the woman with such conviction and such fierce love that water spilled from Dee Dee's eyes.

My Mary reached out and touched the tips of Odessa's fingers. Mary loved the old woman. For this is the power of a wise love wisely given: to transfigure a heart, suddenly and forever.

Miz Odessa Williams died on Tuesday, the twenty-second of December.

It had been a long time coming, but was quick when it came. She died in her sleep and went to the Lord without her dentures.

Quick when it came, I say, because Odessa left us little time to mourn. The funeral had to take place the day after tomorrow, which was Thursday, because Gaines Funeral Home—which was the only mortuary that serviced African Americans—always took Thursdays and weekends off. For this particular week they were closed on Friday as well. No one did business on Christmas day. Therefore, Miz Williams' body had to be prepared for her wake by Wednesday evening.

Moreover, for me this was a week of exhausting distractions. Christmas threw us all into hectic action—what with the Christmas Eve pageant and extra sermons to prepare. My pastoral duties were doubled. Odessa's funeral tripled them.

I ate my Wednesday lunch with my four children. Not brutally, but busily, I mentioned that Miz Williams had died. We were eating soup. This was not an unusual piece of news. The congregation had its share of elderly folks.

I scarcely noticed that Mary stopped eating and was staring into her bowl of soup.

I wiped my mouth and rose from the table.

"Dad?"

"What, Mary. Make it quick."

"Dad?"

"Say it fast. I've got to get back to church."

"Dad," she said, "is it going to snow tomorrow?"

"I don't know. How should I know that?"

"It shouldn't snow."

"But you like snow, especially at Christmas."

In a tiny voice she said, "I want to go to the funeral."

"Fine," I said. "Ask mom to drive you." And I left.

WE HAD A CUSTOM at Grace.

Before a funeral service began, we set the casket immediately in front of the chancel and left it open for about an hour. People came to pay their final respects before rushing off to work. She who had passed away lay with an everlasting patience while the line moved by.

Soon folks started to stay in the church. They unbuttoned their coats and sat down in the pews, waiting for the service to begin. They reminded me of winter birds on telephone wires with their feathers puffed out.

When there were but ten minutes left I robed myself and stood at the church doors in order to greet the family when it arrived in long black limousines.

And so it was on that Christmas Eve at eleven o'clock in the morning. Odessa Williams had no family to speak of. But the courtly Mr. George, Gaines' funeral director, was about to arrive, if not in the hearse, then in his limousine. I opened the door to look for him and found instead my daughter.

She was staring up at a grey, sullen sky.

"Mary?" I said. Then I said, "Do you want to come in?"

"Dad," she whispered as though her news was dreadful, "it's going to snow."

"Come in, come in," I said. "I'll walk with you."

I led Mary up the aisle so that she, too, could pay her respects to Miz Williams.

She looked into the casket and said, "Oh, no," and I looked to see what she was seeing.

Odessa's eyes seemed sewn shut, the lashes the stitching. Her lips were too pale. Her color was a lighter shade than it used to be, false and woody. The bridge of her nose suffered wire glasses set askew. I didn't remember that Odessa wore glasses. Clearly, someone else had perched them there. What belonged to the woman any more? And what did not?

Mary reached to Odessa's fingers, which had been laid in prayer upon her bosom. Mary touched the tip of Odessa's fingers—then snatched back her hand.

"Dad!" she hissed. She looked directly at me, accusing. Her face was crimson. She was fighting tears. "It's going to snow!" she said. "Miz Williams is already cold. They *can't* put her in the grave today! It's Christmas Eve, and it's going to snow on her."

Suddenly Mary buried her face in my robes.

My Mary had met death. It is the end of things. It gave her the knowledge that things *do* have endings— good things, kind and blessed things, things rare and precious. Even the people she loved must have their endings.

I knelt down and drew her small body to myself. For this is the cruelty of the love once wisely given. It will transfigure the heart a second time, when love is torn asunder.

I watched Mary stump down the aisle like a poker soldier. She sat by her mother with her arms folded and her lips drawn into an angry knot. No crying now. No questions anymore. Why should she ask questions when there were no answers?

To THIS DAY I remember the sermon I preached for Odessa's funeral and the Scripture lesson underlying it. Isaiah 9 in the Revised Standard Version, starting at the first verse:

> *Now there will be no gloom for her that was in anguish.*

I described Odessa's gloom. I described the progression of her lung cancer. I described the long, tall woman herself and her absolutes. I described her soul, which was one part scold and one part arrogance, but everywhere faithful.

I have always stuck to the truth when preaching the life of someone who has passed—which requires me to speak of their sins. Sweet eulogies are either vague or false. They have no lasting value for those who mourn. But first to speak of sins, and *then* to speak of Christ's cross and the grace that covers our sins, that alone establishes a lasting comfort and the confidence of heaven. For Jesus' resurrection resurrects those whom he clothes in white robes.

I used the image of a movie theater. Odessa, I said, had been sitting in darkness:

For the people who walked in darkness have seen
a great light; those who dwelt in a land of deep
darkness, on them has the light shined.

This light is certainly not what she saw on the movie screen. Movies are a fiction, a poor representation of the real world. The spiritual world. But at the ending of her life Odessa got up and walked out of the theater, and the light of God's sun—*that* light— nearly blinded her.

Even so is the love and the pure presence of God made manifest among us.

When I had graduated from the seminary, I entered the ministry with a most simplistic notion of the

Gospel. I presented it according to a swift script: "Died and rose again for you," I preached. My job, I thought, was to surprise the parishioners with that phrase. I used illustrations and rhetoric in order to, as it were, sneak up to that repeatable phrase, then gave it to them full bore: "Died and rose again for you"—hey, hey!

But that rote was of little help for anyone.

Loving and living among the people of the neighborhood, experiencing the true nature of the hardships of the poor, led me to the cross. The Jesus scourged, the Jesus whom the general world despised (as it despises the impoverished, blaming them as if poverty were their own fault), the Jesus who loved the poor and the outcasts, the Jesus perishing on the cross—he knows their trouble, and he is their savior. The cross then. It was the cross of the risen Shepherd whom I had met outside Oxford. And Jesus was the farmer who had clucked his flock to follow him. It was to the cross that I led my people. For that sad and glorious event—*that* is the Gospel.

Those citizens who have never truly committed themselves to the poor cannot know how much the poor would rather work. They too yearn for dignity. The underprivileged must stand in lines for half a day: hours and hours without pay. They have no lawyers to argue their cases against unscrupulous landlords. And the police assume them to be criminals. Successful folk call them lazy.

"Pull yourself up by your bootstraps," yes. But I know of no one—rich or poor—who can do so without help. Can anyone raise his own weight merely by grabbing that weight at the shoes with nothing else to lean on? Jesus Christ could not so much as carry his cross.

The lifestyle of that marine who packed his "Menace" could not improve itself except that someone teach him.

While deciding whether they ought to close their doors, the members of Grace Church studied on why the Lord should have placed them in the inner city. They came to realize that they were there to serve the needs of the downtrodden. Grace, then, pledged to be their help and to offer their shoulders as their leaning places.

Therefore we created what we called "The Mission of Grace." We were smart enough to resist the easy route. That is, we did not give handouts. Nor did we give them vouchers for restaurants or for groceries. We did not accept *their* solutions to their problems. Instead, we assessed the problem ourselves and found longer-lasting solutions. We taught them how to buy in bulk, how to cook inexpensively. We showed them how to budget their meager income. We helped them clean their houses. We sent them greeting cards.

In order to support this ministry, I went to Redeemer and spoke about the sheep and the goats, about the King's praise for those who fed the hungry and the thirsty, those who welcomed strangers and who clothed the naked—because the hungry, the thirsty, the stranger, and the naked all were Jesus Christ himself!

I begged Redeemer to see Jesus in the faces of our neighborhood. And Redeemer agreed. But then they wanted to control the money they intended to give. It should be used only for this, they said, and only for that, as if they offered the Mission of Grace a dollar but would not let go of it. *Noblesse oblige.* They planned to remain the nobles while the poor would remain their peasants.

Not all the members of Redeemer thought this way, of course. And in the end they accepted my explanation that giving meant giving completely and allowing those who received the gift to make their own decisions. "All who believed," Luke recorded:

> . . . *were together and had all things in common. They sold their possessions and goods and distributed them to all, as any had need.*

MY DAUGHTER MARY WAS not comforted by my sermon. She stared at the stained glass window behind me, above the altar, and glowered. What to her were Isaiah and prophecy and all the sustaining truths of Christendom? What was heaven to her? Nothing. *Odessa* had been something. Someone very important. You could touch Odessa and fall in love with her. But Odessa was dead.

In Oak Hill Cemetery the people stood in great coats around the casket, shivering. The sky was dark and overcast. In regard for Mary's glum attitude I read of dust and ashes returning to dust and ashes. My tone was more somber than it had been in the sermon, wherein I had promised joy.

When we turned from the grave and walked back to our car, Mary yanked at my sleeve and hissed, "See? It's snowing." A light powder was indeed collecting at the roots of the dried grass.

THAT AFTERNOON I FOUND Mary lying facedown on her bed.

"Mary," I said, "do you want us to get another Mary?"

As it happened, she was to take the role of the Virgin in the pageant to be played at church in the evening.

"No," she said with some force. She said, "*I* am Mary."

WE DROVE THROUGH DARKNESS to the church. The snow lay a loose inch on the pavement. It swirled in snow devils behind a passing car. It fell in dusty cones below the streetlamps.

The church was filled with light and noise. A loud hubbub had taken the place of the low, funereal murmurs of the morning. Black folk were greeting one another. Parents stood in knots, chattering and covering the laughter in their mouths. Children darted past them in bathrobes (the shepherds) and in white choir robes (the angels).

But Mary and I moved like ghosts through this glad company.

Soon the sounds subsided. The little actors huddled in their proper places. I sat down in the second pew on the right-hand side. The sanctuary lights dimmed, while the chancel remained radiant. The pageant began.

A sixth-grade boy walked to the pulpit and shouted, "Fear not. For behold, I bring tidings of great joy! For unto you is born this day in the city of David a Savior, which is Christ the Lord."

Angels went forward and giggled and scratched the air with their fingers, greeting their parents. They sang, "Gloria!" Then came back down.

Two kids carried a wooden manger up the aisle. Behind them came Joseph and Mary, both Marys. My Mary carried a floppy black doll in white diapers. When the manger was set in precisely the place where Miz Williams' casket had been set, my daughter took baby Jesus by the hair and dropped him on the manger's straw. Then she knelt, her bottom lip stuck out.

Joseph stood behind her. A severe carpenter.

Shepherds ran up, and grinned at Jesus, and lowed like cows, and brayed like goats.

I watched as Mary put out her pointer finger and poked at the doll. All at once, as though she'd made a sudden decision, she yanked the Jesus-doll out by his toe like a dishrag, stood up, and marched out of the chancel and into my little office.

People made mild, maternal sounds. The rhythm of the pageant faltered. The pianist stopped playing.

I bit my knuckles and yearned to go to her, to hold her, to protect her from all evil.

In a moment the child emerged carrying nothing at all. She skipped—she skipped!—up the steps and into the chancel and knelt and squinted, trying to find me in the darkness.

So the pageant kicked into high gear.

All the children gathered and in a wonderful harmony sang:

> *Go tell it on the mountain*
> *Over the hills and everywhere;*
> *Go tell it on the mountain,*
> *That JESUS CHRIST IS BORN!*

The chancel lights dimmed. Candle flames were passed from member to member along the pews.

Then the deep black voices of the congregation joined the children.

Silent night, holy night,
All is calm, all is bright
Round yon Virgin, mother and child,
Holy infant so tender and mild,
Sleep in heavenly peace,
Sleep in heavenly peace.

And upon the third verse, Dee Dee Lawrence took wing:

Silent night, holy night,
Son of God, love's pure light
Radiant beams from your holy face,
With the dawn of redeeming grace,
Jesus, Lord, at thy birth,
Jesus, Lord, at thy birth.

As we drove home, Mary sat against me in the car. Snow blew lightly across the windshield and closed us in a cotton privacy. No longer was I troubled by the cold winter's snow.

Mary said, "Dad?"

"What, Mary?"

"Dad, that wasn't Jesus in the manger. It was just a raggedy old doll."

My Mary—with the eyes of a realist. Death had revealed to her its hard truths.

"Dad?"

"What?"

"The manger was empty, on account of Jesus goes up and down. He was born here, but then he zoomed back to heaven, right?"

"Right." Oh, it was good to hear my child talking happily again.

"Dad?"

"What?"

"It wasn't Miz Williams in that box. Just a big doll. Jesus zoomed up. Miz Williams zoomed up right along with him."

THE SEMINARY TRAINED ME. But Grace was my teacher. By grace my feet grew beautiful.

Fourteen

IN THE YEARS TO COME the congregation began to spill out of the pews. At first we set folding chairs down the aisle. Finally we were forced to add a second service. People began to pray their own prayers out loud during the worship service. No matter that their prayers were emotional and long, and the service longer than it had been.

White folks began to visit us.

The Mission of Grace worked out of the old parsonage, into which I moved my office. I bought two comfortable chairs, and there I did my counseling.

Listen, pastor. Listen and watch.

Over and over again, I was taught by the Holy Spirit through the dark congregation of Grace Church. This is how I learned the value of telling stories while preaching:

EVEN DOWN TO THIS day, preaching has unnerved me.

Saturday nights I could hardly sleep. I got up from bed early Sunday morning—about five o'clock in the morning—and drove through darkness to the church. There I paced, hurtling up and down the aisle, finding thoughts, ordering those thoughts, cudgeling words from my brain, and going to the bathroom several times before the sun began to touch the eastern stained-glass windows. For me it was a terrible thing, to preach. Not only did I fear that I might ruin the proclamation of the gospel, but I also trembled to stand before an "audience" alone. It was my custom not to use notes.

Then came my first Easter morning.

Perhaps an hour before the service, children began to show up. Ages four to twelve. Not a single parent. The children laughed and shouted and blustered through the church, shattering my concentration.

Finally, in desperation I gathered them, the kids and the teens, in the sanctuary and told them to sit down. They did, facing me, scrubbed and smiling and awaiting . . . something.

Now, I had told stories to my brother in bed at night. I had made up fictions in school, which my teachers called "lies" when they found me out. I had long been writing stories. Had won awards with my tales.

Therefore, it was a story that leaped into my mind. And what better story than the Easter passion?

The story started with the Last Supper. Jesus was

sitting and eating with his disciples. Peter wore a tank top, stuffing himself with lamb chops. Grease ran into his beard. But Jesus, I told the children, was sad. I drew a sad face. So did the children. Children are quick to respond with moods, even before they know the reasons.

John said, "What's the matter?" John was so close to Jesus that he could lay his head upon Jesus' shoulder.

Jesus said, "Someone's going to rat me out to the Man."

Now, Jesus was the hero of the story. Of course the children frowned.

Worse, Jesus told them that the rat was one of his friends, one of the people sitting and eating with him.

"Me?" said Peter. "Not *me,* Lord. Hey, John!" he said. "Ask the Lord who it is."

Jesus answered and said, "Not you. It's Judas."

So Judas was the bad guy. Right away he got up and sneaked out into the night.

I kept on telling the story. Jesus was going to die.

But heroes don't die! No, Jesus would get out of this somehow.

When he got to Gethsemane, he threw himself on the ground. He scratched the ground with his fingers. And Peter, who was supposed to guard the Lord, fell asleep.

The children frowned. Peter wasn't a great guy either.

Jesus prayed to God because really bad soldiers were going to whip his back and make him carry the beam of the cross on his back.

Then here came Judas with a bunch of cops. So that the cops could pick Jesus from the crowd, Judas kissed him. *Kissed* him.

So the cops cuffed the Lord and dragged him to the judge. And the judge said, "Guilty! Give him the maximum punishment!"

That's when soldiers took out their whips. These whips had nails. The nails cut Jesus' back till he was bleeding. No matter. Bleeding wasn't enough.

No, no, heroes don't die.

But the soldiers took spikes and hammered them through Jesus' hands and into the wooden beam. Then they raised the wooden beam—with Jesus hanging on it—up onto a post and left him there to die.

While I said this, I lifted up my arms and pretended to be Jesus. With my arms up I slumped. I made my voice scritchy, on account of Jesus' chest closed when he grew weak and could only hang. Then I said that the spikes were his friends for a little while, because when he found a little strength he pulled himself up and he could breathe again.

The children gaped.

Finally Jesus could not hold himself up any longer. His arms stretched until his shoulders popped. The air went out of him. He suffocated. Jesus died.

It was about this time when the children's parents started to arrive, dressed in their Easter best. When they saw their sons and daughters, the adults wondered that they were so sad.

They were supposed to be glad. Hadn't they gone looking for Easter eggs? Hadn't someone hidden the eggs for them to find?

Ah, *that's* why the kids had come so early to church. To hunt eggs.

But now they sat confused. Because heroes aren't supposed to die.

I don't remember what I'd planned to preach on. But I do remember what it was I did do, what I had no choice but to do.

I told the rest of the story. How Mary Magdalene felt just like the children. She stood by the grave of her Lord. She was crying. Then here came a man who said to her, "Why are you crying? What's the matter?"

Well, because her tears blurred what she was seeing, she didn't know that it was Jesus himself, her hero.

She said, "Somebody carried my Lord away. I want to find him."

Then Jesus said, "Mary. Herman. Dee Dee. Timmy."

Just hearing his voice made Mary jump for joy. She knew! All at once she knew that this man was Jesus. He had gotten up from his grave. He was alive!

So, that was an Easter truly.

And the Holy Spirit had taught me how to preach. With stories.

This, you see, is how inner-city folks listen best. They don't tend to read bulletins. But what they experience, they remember. And that is the power of a tale well told. It invites the hearers into it as if they were the characters themselves. Imagination surrounds them with the story. It is their whole world for a while.

Once I heard a black preacher say, "Today my text will be . . . the Bible." Then he told its story starting with Adam and Eve, all the way through to Jesus.

"Start low," the black preacher once said to me, "start low. Go high. Sit down."

AN OLD MAN, A truly enormous man named Arthur Bias, died under my watch.

I visited him in the hospital to pray with his wife, Musetta, with his son, Arthur Jr., and with his friends in the room before me.

In those days I read my prayers formally from a book called *The Pastor's Companion*.

"Almighty and eternal God, dear, faithful heavenly Father, comfort Arthur. Strengthen him. Spare him through thy great mercy. Help him out of all agony and distress. Release him in thy grace. Take him to thee, into thy kingdom—"

At which point Musetta cried, "AMEN!" and blew me right out of my book. A host of voices boomed in chorus, "Jesus, Jesus!"

Never thereafter did I pray as I had learned to pray

in the seminary. Just now I had been taught otherwise. I prayed *ex corde*, from my heart, expecting folks to support my praying with their ringing dialogue.

As long as he lived, Arthur embraced me in a circle of peace.

"Rev? You want t' toss a line t'mornin'?" he would say.

It doesn't take living in the inner city to know that there's a whole load of folk most angry and most particular that others should feel the brunt of their anger. Or maybe the world is angrier than it used to be and looking for doorsteps to dump their anger on, and the handiest porch gets the pile. Are people less content? Quicker to take offense and slower to forgive?

When we pastors complained one summer that the neighborhood swimming pool had been left dry and chain-locked—though other children splashed in other pools—a certain citizen wrote a letter to the editor: "If you people would take care of your own and keep it clean, you would deserve our attention, and we *would* open it for your children."

What happened to plain fellowship?

Arthur Bias spoke in a deep voice. He was large-jowled, a slow-striding man. He wore his white hair cut close to his head. Arthur had been a policeman before he retired.

The man bottom-fished. Therefore, so did I. It took less energy to let the hook sink down from its bobber, a grub for bait a bare inch above the muck. Or else an angleworm he'd dug from his garden. Or a cricket. Caught catfish with bacon. Bullheads with a bit of cheese.

Arthur sat in a lawn chair. Lit a pipe. Slit his eyes. Stayed silent, musing for a good long while. The drone of the flies softened our brains to drowsiness. The old man sighed at the goodness of an uncomplicated life.

He dozed, making a moist buzzing in his nose. Then he'd wake to the tug of a fish, twitch his eyebrows, and reel in his dinner. Then he would talk in rolling tones, and his voice was for me a benediction. His past had been constructed of common things. He never desired more than that. And he himself was more than contented. He was kind.

"Ahmmm," he murmured through the vast passages of his sinuses. "Never did pull mah service revolver more'n a few times, no. Mostly Ah never had to. Made mah wishes known in other ways."

He had walked a beat in the core of the city. His leather heels cracked on the sidewalk. He could call everyone by name—renters and owners, shopkeepers, garbage men, families in shotgun houses, and people in the projects. He had known them since they were pups on their mothers' knees.

Arthur used moral persuasion. And the authority of his massive size. And the badge. The gun, the vomit of wrath and death, only when guns were drawn on him.

"Tell you what," he said, squinting over the river, "even them long-legged boys and them gum-snappin' girls-ud heed me—on account of they mamas. Ahmmm, ha-ha, oh yes! Hoo. Mama'ud willow-switch 'em when they hied 'emselvs home, if'n I axed as much. 'Cause we been knowin' each the t'other since we was singin' in the church when we was chirren.

"Well, an' I didn't care none if'n them boys liked me or no. But I tell you what. They liked me."

Arthur made his lawn chair bulge both back and bottom. The man made the city civil. He laughed, his shoulders heaving and his stomach seismic, and I felt the very mantle of the earth respond.

When he lay dying in Deaconess Hospital, Arthur asked for green beans. He explained that the best way to cook green beans was in bacon grease, or else with sausages boiled to the point of popping.

He spoke about food with as much affection as he had spoken about the people on his beat, or as he had about his wife. It was all one, and all of it sufficient. That which he had, he cherished. That which he didn't have, God saw no reason to give him.

In the end Arthur lifted his eyes to a corner in the ceiling. "Musetta," he said in his deep voice, "Ah'ma sorry you can't see her. It's my grandmama, watchin' and waitin' for me to come on home."

Reverend? You want to toss a line t'mornin'?

Long afternoons at the edge of a sleepy river were no

less than Eden. Arthur was Adam. And faith is peace.
And I wandered in his garden.

IT WAS DURING THE synodical wars that I had learned
to recognize the countenance of faith.

I saw it in the faces of the professors who had been
fired as heretics, those who had had their names stricken
from the synodical roster.

Thanne and I were attending a convocation held
in a Chicago suburb. Foremost on the agenda were
two questions: How could a few churches finance and
support the seminary in exile, whose students had left
the Missouri Synod's doctrinaire seminary and whose
professors had been fired? And: Should the churches
form a new body of Lutherans? Members of the
Seminex faculty showed up, of course, for the convocation.

The meeting was bright with hope—and more
crowded than I had expected.

It happened that Thanne and I stepped into an
elevator already occupied by four men. The doors slid
shut and I glanced around. These men were doctors of
theology, four of the faculty that had been given the
bum's rush out of their offices and out of their houses.
They went, knowing nothing of their future.

Nevertheless, they stood beside us in perfect peace.

Trust and fearlessness were in their faces. I had never seen faith so clearly incarnated before.

I was moved to be one among their number.

In the end we elected to become a church of our own: the AELC, the Association of Evangelical Lutheran Churches.

We sang the inception:

The Church's one foundation
Is Jesus Christ, her Lord;
She is his new creation
By water and the Word.
From heaven he came and sought her
To be his holy bride;
With his own blood he bought her,
And for her life he died. . . .

Arthur Bias carried me yet one level higher. Gently he offered me to share his faith, and he encircled me in peace.

Fifteen

That novel which I had been writing since fulfilling my tasks at Redeemer—the manuscript which I entitled *The Book of the Dun Cow*—was finally placed with Harper & Row. It was published in 1978. In 1980 it came out in paperback, for which Thanne and I were paid a substantial advance. Moreover, some benefactor sent us a cashier's check for $2000.

With that money I bought a small green Toyota pick-up truck.

It was possible now to buy a house in the inner city in order to make a full commitment to Grace and to its neighborhood. So we went shopping.

All the houses we looked at were far out of our price range.

Then we saw a newspaper article announcing that an auction would be held for a house which the city had completely refurbished in order to be a model for what federal monies could do to other neighborhood houses.

They were, the article said, taking bids.

Given our financial straits, we bid what we could, five hundred dollars. Surely, this was too low to win.

But the God whom I thought I had lost during that first year in graduate school had never lost me.

After about a month we received a telephone call from the city. Our bid had taken the house. In fact, the caller said glumly, ours had been the only bid.

Two stories had that house. Four bedrooms upstairs. Two heating and cooling units, one for each floor. Downstairs, luxury: a large living room with a full fireplace. A *foyer*, for heaven's sake. Kitchen, dinner nook, an enormous dining room, a family room, two bathrooms, a full basement, and a wide and windowed front porch. Oh, what God hath wrought!

The members of Grace helped us move. The men drove trucks. The women washed the windows, swept out old dust, and generally cleaned the house, singing all the while. There was a library across the street and tennis courts and a municipal park to the east.

The house was a mere five blocks from the church.

There were, of course, drawbacks.

Matt's bicycle was stolen from the porch.

On summer nights teens and young adults parked their cars in front of the library and turned their boom-boxes up, their thundering rhythms boom-booming against our house, and the people dancing, shouting, laughing, gambling, smoking pot.

Once our youngest daughter stood on the front lawn watching one woman shooting at another woman, who was racing away with her skirt high above her thighs. Little Talitha was enjoying the show.

"You come back, bitch, an' Ah'ma gonna keel you!"

I dashed out to my child, grabbed her up (to her dismay), and ran back into the house.

CHERYL LAWRENCE SENT A friend of hers to my church office, convinced that I could set the woman straight.

The woman's name was Rita Cooksey. She was furious with the man who used to be her boyfriend.

Rita was as beautiful as the night—tall, slender, an even and narrow face, her complexion polished walnut.

I seem to remember that she came to me in twilight.

After introductions and after she told me her story, Rita revealed the intensity of her anger. She pulled a small pistol from her purse. She had every intention of shooting the wretch.

But she was also ready to believe injunctions of the Lord—and did finally obey them.

Perhaps a month later, Rita joined a class I was teaching for those who hoped to become members of our church.

Philip Lawrence was in the class.

So was Linda Hudson. She'd just moved back to her family in Evansville. In Milwaukee Linda had kept a safe-house for men of the Black Power Movement, but their sexism nettled her. She closed the house and moved back home.

Rita *did* become a member of Grace, as well as an earnest student of the Bible. At the same time she began to feel a whole new urging of the Lord Jesus. Now and again a particular verse would stand out for her. I mean that the printed words themselves seemed to arise in a bold black.

What she read she communicated to the rest of us as though she were Christ's mediator.

IN TIME I BECAME aware that gossip was riddling the congregation.

There were two women's societies: the Altar Guild and the Semper Fidelis. Each had grown hostile to the other. Hostility was expressed in backbiting, and I despaired of changing them.

But God slapped me into his service.

It has always been my habit to preach on the lessons long established for every Sunday of the church year. For the first half of the church year the gospel lessons walk us through the story of the life of Christ. For the second half they attend to his miracles, his healings, and his teachings. At the same time, the Epistle lessons come with instructions and promises written by the apostles.

While I felt helpless to reform the women of their gossiping, this Epistle lesson appeared:

> *For the whole law is fulfilled in one word, "You shall love your neighbor as yourself." But if you bite and devour one another, take heed lest you consume one another.*

Ah, God, then I had no choice. I was bound now to preach the sermon that would lay their sin open, and to charge them with breaking the fifth commandment. I was called to be their Jeremiah.

All week long I suffered the prospect of wounding my beloved. I couldn't sleep. Food tasted like sand. I'm afraid I sinned myself by barking at my children.

And on Sunday morning sweat kept trickling down my spine.

But I did what I had to do. I preached:

> *Words kill. Gossip is no less violent than a knife, even if the sinner should never confront her target and draw blood. Gossip attacks rather her reputation. She cannot thereafter move freely among society. People are offended by her loathsome presence.*

"Let's say that a person walks out of the room. While she's gone, another person fills the rest with words about her bad character. Now let's say the person who was talked about returns to the room. Suddenly she is not the person that she was. Others look at her with contempt. Her new identity is contemptuous. What she had been has been murdered.

The Gospel lesson for that same Sunday offered forgiveness. I seized on that: Luke 9:51 and following.

When people did not receive Jesus, the disciples said, "Lord, do you want us to bid fire come down from heaven and consume them?" This is what should happen to those who reject the humility of the Christ. But Jesus turned and rebuked the disciples. Soon he would, he said, take the fires upon himself, and they would kill him on the cross. His death—the death of the Word Made Flesh—in place of the deaths of those who, by a word of gossip, had themselves killed others.

So I ended the sermon with a loud cry of forgiveness.

I sat down in the chancel with a sigh of enormous relief. I had done what God had asked.

After church I went downstairs into the basement fellowship hall.

Behind the kitchen door, which was cracked enough that I could hear them, several women were talking about my sermon.

"What was the matter with pastor?" they asked.

"I don't know," they answered.

"Well, he's got some sorta thorn up his butt."

Even so, even so.

I COUNSELED THE DEFEATED, and they left still defeated.

I counseled couples about to marry. I told them that romantic love would not sustain them, that it should be their public covenant that held them together through the trials of communal living. I told them that pride would ride a high horse, demanding more from their spouses than their spouses could reasonably give. Soon sin would cause them pain. I said that it was *then* that Jesus could enter the marriage, by their confession and the forgiveness the Lord could empower.

But they would smile and nod and lock fingers and whisper to one another that *their* love was stronger than the loves I knew.

I pleaded with them to call me. I would marry them. I wanted to keep their marriage whole when they ran into difficulty.

They left my office unconcerned. And they wept at the wedding. And I smiled.

I counseled couples whose marriage had turned sour, who were on the way to divorce. If there'd been abuse, I worked hardest with the abuser. He must humble himself before the Lord, before me, and before his wife, and beg forgiveness. I explained to the wife what forgiveness looked like.

The husband left my office with assurances that he could indeed confess.

"Abjectly?" I asked.

"I'm dust and ashes," he said. "Better believe it, reverend."

Within the week he was back in my office.

"It's *her* turn," he snarled. "I *said* I'm sorry, but it didn't do no good."

Days later, the wife came running to our house, sobbing. She had a swelling bruise under her eye. She was most particularly afraid for her baby whom she'd left behind in her rush to escape.

I left the woman with Thanne and walked the short way to her house, ever and ever, forever tense.

Her husband, the father of the infant, did not answer my knock. But the door was open so I walked in. He had the baby in his arms. I asked for it, and he gave it to me. My duty, my pastoral duty.

One night a boy called me up and begged me to come over. His father and his older brother were fighting.

Duties. My pastoral duties.

I sat in my office alone, dispirited.

"Almighty God, what do you *want* of me?"

A song that Dee Dee Lawrence had once sung began to sing in my mind:

*Why should I feel discouraged, why should the
    shadows come,*
*Why should my heart be lonely and long for heaven
    and home,*
*When Jesus is my portion, my constant friend is
    he.*
His eye is on the sparrow. . . .

I prayed, "They are all your sparrows, my God. Yours! I give them all to you."

And I prayed as once I prayed years and years ago: "Love me. Love me. Love me."

Sixteen

WE WERE TRAVELING SOUTH ON Interstate 55, thirty-five of us in a single bus.

The Sounds of Grace were off on a weeklong tour: New Orleans in Louisiana, Texas, Arkansas, Missouri, and Illinois. I was awake. The rest were sleeping. We'd left Evansville early that Saturday morning. Our first concert took place the night before in Memphis, and folks were tired.

The Grace Notes, it turned out, were not enough for Grace Church. We formed another choir, which we named "The Sounds of Grace." Students from Evansville University had begun to worship with us. They wanted to know what they could do for the church.

Cheryl Lawrence knew.

These students and our youth and our children and their parents proved to make a glorious sound. They sang gospel songs with power and a swaying vigor.

At Concordia I had myself traveled with that school's chorus to other cities and other churches. I'd learned the routine. Now, therefore, it occurred to me that voices like these should be heard abroad. So: Cheryl and I planned to take them abroad.

I wrote and telephoned pastors in order to dot our tour with venues. We asked the congregations to bed us in exchange for song. They all agreed.

It was on this tour that God taught the choir the ministry for which they had been made: black ambassadors to white churches.

Early Sunday we were welcomed by the people who had promised to put us up for the night. Choir members unloaded the bus not only of luggage, but also of their robes and their instruments. It became our practice to rehearse an hour before the concert. A drummer, and bass guitar, and a piano. Cheryl played the piano on that tour. Herman Thomas Jr. directed.

We glorified that Lutheran worship service.

The pastor said to me, "If only I'd known that the Sounds were this good, I would have invited *all* the churches."

In fact, I had told him this choir was outstanding. But really, how good could a little inner city congregation be?

Already on Monday evening, New Orleans began to celebrate Fat Tuesday. The members of the choir, especially the young girls, scattered throughout the crowd, jumping and catching baubles. I suffered anxiety. What if they got lost or hurt? But nothing bothered these bubbling, self-confident teens. They came back with loads of plastic geegaws, shrill necklaces, hard candy.

Tuesday morning we boarded the bus and took off for Houston, stopping to swim the sea at Galveston.

In Houston the pastor made the same stunned compliments. "If only I had known . . ."

Thanne and I and the kids stayed the night in the pastor's house.

After the children had gone to sleep, Reverend Steinke asked where we were to perform in Dallas.

I told him, "At Pastor Rasp's church."

Steinke pinched his lips and frowned. "You could," he told us, "run into trouble there."

He said no more.

But when we boarded the bus, Cheryl, Phil, Herman Thomas, and Thanne and I gathered in the front of the bus for a quick conference. Cheryl was nervous. She too had been warned about the church in Dallas.

We prayed and left it up to God.

When we arrived, the choir was awestruck. This church was more than a single building. It was a campus. Gracious trees grew within a stone-walled enclosure. Flowers lined the walkways. The air itself seemed perfumed.

While the choir members went about their regular routine, Cheryl and I met with the pastoral intern (a third-year seminary student), who sat behind his desk and steepled his fingers. We explained our program. Gina Moore would enter the sanctuary first and walk up the aisle singing "For God So Loved the World" *a cappella*. Then Timmy Moore would follow her repeating the verse in his cushion of a tenor voice. Finally the whole choir would enter clapping, quick-stepping up the aisle in a jubilant rhythm.

The intern shuddered.

Between pieces, I said, I would ravel out a story and preach.

The intern said, "How long will this take?"

Cheryl said, "Fifty minutes. Maybe an hour."

He nodded, understanding the time, then shook his head to the possibility.

"We'll give you twenty-five minutes at most. This is Ash Wednesday. *Our* choir is scheduled to sing. Rev. Rasp will do the preaching. You can present your program after the service and the benediction. If you go too long, people will grow restless."

I was dumbfounded at these prohibitions. We'd have to cut most of the music, slash my preaching, and rewrite everything.

At that moment Rev. Rasp in a grey suit, greying hair, and a handsome face, floated into the room. He sailed in front of us, looked, then sailed on out again—all without a single word.

The intern's next comment downright angered me.

"Until you sing," he said, "we'll seat you in the balcony."

That sanctuary was cavernous. Altar and chancel and the pastors would be as far below us as though we sat on the roof of a ten-story building.

And we were black!

This is the trouble about which we'd been warned. When contacting Dallas, I must have neglected to mention that The Sounds of Grace was an African American choir.

When we left the intern behind his desk, I burned with the humiliation.

Cheryl said, "Easy, pastor, easy. We can do this."

She, of course, had been handling racism all her life.

We selected four pieces of music. I was determined to climb into Rev. Rasp's high pulpit between each piece and give the congregation what-for.

While Cheryl went into the sanctuary for rehearsal, I stormed back and forth in the library—a library! A whole building unto itself!

Suddenly Herman burst through the door and threw himself in a chair. He was crying. He said, "I don't want to be here. Let's go. Let's just get on the bus and go."

He told me what had happened.

During the rehearsal, Tony Calhoun reached to the altar to catch something before it fell. Out of the darkness at the back of the church, a loud voice shouted with threat, "Don't you *touch* that!"

Rev. Rasp had been lurking, observing.

Herman knew the spirit that issued that threat.

"Tell Cheryl. We got to get away from here."

I cannot say otherwise, but that it was the Holy Spirit who gave me words I would not have uttered five minutes before.

I kneeled down before Herman and said, "Of all the places we will ever sing, we *have* to sing for this church."

Herman said, "Why?"

And I said, "Because they don't know love."

I asked him to speak to the choir. Warn them. But tell them that this was our most important concert.

Herman left. I started to change my angry words into proclaiming words: "God *is* love."

Thanne brought in a tray of supper for me.

As she was setting it down, *I* burst into tears. I fell on her shoulders and sobbed.

So then: in the balcony. Herman and I sat side by side. He nudged me and pointed to a sentence that someone had etched into the pew with a ballpoint pen. It said, "I don't know this." Herman nodded at me.

Pastor Rasp preached on seven questions answered by the cross. The first question: "Are you a sinner? Do you need forgiveness?"

"Yes!" he yelled. "Pour contempt on all your pride!"

Then it was our turn.

Gina Moore walked up the aisle singing in a supernal soprano: "For God so loved the world . . ."

Once she had gained her place in the chancel, Timmy walked after her, likewise singing, "For God so loved the world, that he gave his only begotten son, that whoever believes in him should have everlasting life."

I had told the choir not to sway, not to take on Baptist strains. Honor these people right where they were.

I sat behind the choir when they sang. I couldn't see past them. The pulpit stood on a pedestal, four steps up from the chancel floor. Between each piece I climbed the pulpit and spoke (briefly) a series of stories of love.

The first time, I saw the congregation fixed in their seats, wondering at this spectacle. The second time they were leaning forward. The third time they were standing.

The last song was "Soon and Very Soon." The choir began to recess. In spite of my request, Timmy lifted his voice into a Baptist jubilation, and the choir was clapping. When they'd drained out into the aisle, I saw why. People were reaching out their hands, taking the hands of the choir, patting their shoulders.

I was the last to recess. To my astonishment, the whole congregation filed from their pews and came behind me—clapping to our rhythm.

They followed us all the way into the changing room.

"We needed this," they said. "Oh, we needed this."

THAT, THEN, WAS THE mission for which God had formed his choir.

Herman said, "God wants us to break down the walls of racism. To sleep in the beds of white houses. And to love white Christians."

The church's one foundation
Is Jesus Christ her Lord.

Seventeen

ONE OF OUR WHITE VISITORS wondered whether she could join Grace. She was an elderly woman given to daily acts of kindness.

I put her request on the agenda for our next church council meeting.

When other business had been completed, we turned to this new topic.

Even before we began to discuss it, Kevin Stewart's expression went quizzical.

He said, "We've always had white members, haven't we?"

The comment surprised me. No, we hadn't. From its beginning Grace had been African American. Several of its *pastors* had been white. Not its members.

Then I interpreted his words to mean that Grace had always been open to anyone: whites, gay folk, the unspeakably poor.

What he said closed the discussion.

The council voted, and the woman was in.

Perhaps a year later she told me what she thought was a pretty funny joke.

She said that she'd thought that the stained glass windows were dirty. (And what did that mean? That blacks don't keep their building as clean as she would?) But she didn't consider it her place to wash them until she actually belonged to Grace.

Straightway after she'd been received into membership, she brought a bucket, filled it with soapy water, found a ladder, and scrubbed the glass mercilessly.

"But," she told me, "they weren't dirty at all, ha ha. That's the way they were made, ha ha."

No joke, really. An unconscious characterization of inner city blacks.

Another woman, well-dressed, made the same request. Her family had owned the newspaper in town. It had been in her family for generations. But she'd sold it and entered the upper class. She was sure that she would be welcomed with open arms on account of the good that her money would do.

"Wait one year," I told her. "If you learn how the congregation can to serve *you*, then join."

Humble thyself before the Lord, and he will exalt you.

One day this well-dressed woman went to visit Larry Johnson in his recycling yard. It looked like a dump, except that real dumps collect garbage to bury it, while Larry's dump collected garbage in order to give it new life again.

Larry received her with a genuine affection. Spontaneously he hugged her. She responded with such love and gratitude that it was no more than a week before she joined.

MIZ ALLOUISE STORY'S HOUSE took a fresh coat of white paint every year. That house was a monument to discipline, frugality, and sanitation. Her green lawn was a stark contrast to the mess surrounding it.

Miz Story lived on the southeast corner of Line and Canal Streets. Doc's Liquor Store did its business several houses away. At night men would come into the trashy lot immediately north of her property and piss their beer into the ground.

Yet she remained right where she was. Miz Story was a stubborn woman. She had an honorable history. Her husband, Nat Story, had built a reputation as a fine trombone jazzman. At Easter sunrise services—which were held at the edge of the Ohio River—he would blow Gabriel's horn exactly as the golden sun burst over the horizon.

Why, then, should she not keep house where she and Nat had lived together?

I believed that she *meant* for her model house to remain on Canal just to prove that even a drunk could change his ways and prosper.

One day in summer she showed me a letter she had received from the office of city planning. The letter announced that the city intended to purchase all the buildings around Line and Canal in order to demolish them. Two businessmen had elected to put a shopping center on that land. The city told her—it didn't ask, it *told* her—that it would buy her house at fair market value.

She said, "I want to die in my own home."

"Do you want to fight this thing?" I asked.

"Yes. Of course."

"Can I help?"

Allouise always refused help. She refused to be dependant of any except herself. But this threat was frightening enough that she said, "Yes."

In those days I wrote a weekly column in the Evansville Scripps Howard newspaper.

Would she mind if I argued her case in public?

In public. Then *everyone* would know her private business.

I said that they might not have to, if first I forewarned city planning that, should they not drop their proposal, *then* I would expose them in a column decrying the city's heartlessness.

Miz Story agreed with that plan.

I arranged a meeting with the superintendent of the planning committee.

I explained to him the necessity of allowing Mrs. Allouise Story to stay right where she was.

"Mrs. Story? Who's she?"

He lacked the knowledge of the people whom he planned to displace.

I gave him her address. I told him who the woman was: a teacher before she retired. A nurse before that. A graduate of the Tuskegee Institute, and the wife of Nat Story. I said that her house was made in the image of God.

He hadn't heard of a Mrs. Allouise Story.

"I write a column in the newspaper," I said.

"A widely read column," he said.

"Do your 'business men' have the financing to build?"

"What?"

"Are they solvent?"

"Well, no. But once they get the go-ahead, they'll sell shares—"

"But before that, sir, there is no need to bulldoze her house?"

"Yes. Well. There are procedures. . . ."

"I'm not asking anything unreasonable. But if the Department of City Planning insists on going forward, I will make the project public and create enough sympathy that citizens will turn against the DCP. Promise me that you will wait."

"Well. Well, then. I'll see what I can do."

MIZ STORY TOOK SICK. She found herself unable to lift her garage door. When I visited her she rubbed and rubbed with one hand, the other hand laid on her knee. The doctors in Evansville could not diagnose the affliction. She was reduced to a wheelchair. Therefore she bought an airline ticket to fly to the Mayo Clinic in Rochester, Minnesota.

She took her "bumbershoot" with her. She said it was to stab people out of the way so she could wheel on through.

The physicians at the Mayo Clinic diagnosed her condition as neurasthenia.

Before she returned to Evansville, I myself was laid up in the hospital. X-rays had shown spots on my right lung. Dr. Waddel prescribed surgery to excise the lower lobe of that lung.

While I waited for that procedure, I received a letter from the DCP. They offered to sell Mrs. Story's house to Grace for one dollar, but we would have to move the building to some plot closer to the church.

It aggrieved me. I was helpless in the hospital. Mrs. Story was giving up the fight. She was, she said, dying.

She sold the house.

Soon she too was placed in the hospital.

When I could, I visited her. She was trying to eat, holding a spoon in her fist like a child. She kept spilling the food down her hospital gown before it reached her mouth.

I slumped heavily into a chair. We gazed at each other for a while, neither of us smiling, both of us infirm.

Miz Story said, "What goes around comes around." Her face hung slack on one side. Her skin was mealy. "The only way to beat old age," she said, "is to die young."

"I tell them how to lay me down," she sighed. Allouise never sighed. "I tell them how to turn me over, how to sit me up. They think I'm a meddling old woman because I choose to keep my knees covered up. *I* choose. I have a girl who comes and writes my letters for me."

"But God is good," I said. "He is with you. Comfort yourself, Allouise. Jesus' blood has washed you clean and granted you his salvation. You can believe in the promise of heaven."

Her dull eyes sparked a little fire.

"I don't know about salvation," she said.

"But Jesus' love is certain."

"Maybe for others."

Oh, Allouise! In what pit did she believe herself to be? *Nobody knows the trouble I've seen. . . .*

"Tell me, what *do* you believe?"

She closed the conversation by saying, "I know what's what."

But this woman had been a pillar of the church! She had never gossiped. She had imposed her will wherever she went.

Her will. God's will? This much I knew: Mrs. Allouise Story had refused to be dependent on anyone.

MARY MOORE CAME TO my hospital room with the notion that I needed comforting.

She considered my therapies and the frailty of my body.

She did not know the frailty of my spirit.

Mary said, "Are you mournin' for Miz Story? Is that why you're crying?"

I put my hands to my eyes. I hadn't known that I was crying.

"I'm so sorry that she died," Mary said.

"Oh, well," I said. "Died." I rubbed my face with the heels of my hands. "Mary, can I talk to you?"

"Yes, pastor. What—"

"No, don't ask questions. Just let me talk." I sat up on the edge of my bed. The television was playing nonsense. I asked her to switch it off.

"I'm sorry too," I said. "Someone should hear why." I hesitated, then said, "I am guilty of the woman."

"Pastor—"

"Hush. No. Please. I want to tell the truth. I am the serpent who swallows the living. I—" I took a deep breath. "The city wanted Mrs. Story's house. I wanted her soul—I did, not God—and I am the worse thief for that. I was using her to prove . . . to prove the wholeness of my ministry. That Jesus is here. I wanted to persuade her that God's grace is all. To persuade myself, I think."

I leveled my gaze at Mary so directly that it caused her to back away from this hard man with wild hospital hair.

"Listen," I said. "This is a confession."

"That's all right," she whispered.

"No, it's not all right."

"It really is," Mary said, "all—"

"I wanted her to admit that you can't buy a gift. You can't command it or seek it for yourself. It wouldn't be a gift then, would it? Gifts are free, freely given, a something for a nothing. Only in the knowledge that you have nothing to give back, nothing with which to purchase God's abundance, and that you are, before Christ's cross, an abject failure, a nonentity—only in that confession can you know grace *as* grace.

"Earnestly, earnestly, for three days together I tried to persuade Allouise of these things. For her sake I wanted to submerge her willfulness. Waiting is all, I said. Waiting without complaining or blaming your-self. The waiting—*that,* I said, is faith enough."

Mary said, "Pastor—"

But I couldn't stop. "I demanded that God should come and promise her, say to her, 'Here I am. I am your Lord, my daughter. I am your father and your savior.'"

Then I paused. Mary did not interrupt. Clearly, what I had to say next was my most difficult confession.

"I told myself that my beggings were on behalf of hard Allouise. But now I know that they were mostly for me. If she believed, then *I* could believe. If I succeeded, then I was a proper minister after all. Oh, I was whipping the woman with Jesus for my own sake. I preached that Jesus was sufficient. 'O come, Lord Jesus,' I prayed, 'Come and be our guest—'"

"Pastor Wangerin," Mary said, "I ain't all that smart, but I'm thinkin' you needed to cry before. You got good reasons to cry."

Eli eli lama sabachthani!

My heart's howling sounded to me like one cricket's chirp among ten thousand thousands.

Eighteen

Stella Mayes's sister Marie Lander, née Hopkins, was shorter and a tad meatier than Stella—"Australia." Marie had a laugh that shocked you with its sudden explosion. "Yah-HA!" she laughed. Louder than young boys: "Yah-*HA!*"

Someone might have said that Marie was superstitious. I myself would call her predilections a kind of trust.

Every year on January the second she would bring me a piece of boiled cabbage wrapped in tinfoil. She said it was an amulet. It would bring me good fortune throughout the following year. I neither disputed nor scorned her. I put the bright little package in my billfold and didn't take it out until the next year when she brought a freshly boiled bit of cabbage.

Marie believed in hands of healing. She suffered violent headaches. When she did, she would seek me out and ask me to lay my hands on her head. I stood behind her and did as she asked. I prayed a prayer over her no less genuine than any I prayed on my own behalf.

And she was healed.

You can't test such a healing. She didn't have crutches to throw down. But you could believe the woman's own declaration that the headaches went away.

Her sister practiced a different sort of art.

Mary Moore, Stella's daughter, cannot have been more than twelve years old when she heard a low, continual murmuring in the night. The girl slipped from her bed and sneaked to the kitchen, whence the murmuring came. She peeped around the doorjamb and saw her mother sitting at a table before a black and burning candle. Stella was feeding strands of human hair into the flame. They critched and crackled, while Stella repeated a spell (or so it seemed) which Mary could not decipher.

She told me that the experience had haunted her long thereafter. She never brought the subject up to Stella. She kept it buried within her heart.

DURING MY TENURE AT Grace, Mary Moore committed herself to seeking out her heritage. She combed libraries and city data banks for birth announcements and obituaries, actually piecing together bits of history. She focused on Hopkinsville, Kentucky, in which her previous generations had made their homes.

Then she had a midnight vision. A light-skinned man stood in the bedroom doorway, gazing at her. The man walked to the foot of her bed and waggled his finger as if saying, "No. Don't do this." It seemed to her that there was some secret she should not unravel.

It was then that she came somewhat fearfully to me. What did the apparition signify? Should she stop looking?

A light-skinned man with a narrow nose, she said.

Once again I did not gainsay the truth of the vision. There are things in this world too numinous to explain or else to deny.

Mary obeyed and quit her investigations.

In the cool autumn of that year, her great uncle passed away, leaving his old Hopkinsville house empty. If it could be, it would be sold, though it was sadly dilapidated.

Before they could decide on a sale, Mary and a male relative drove down to see what might be saved.

She told me that she was working through a back room when she pulled a wide, flat drawer from her great uncle's dresser. She pulled it too far from its tracks and dropped it to the floor. A slew of daguerreotype photographs slipped out like playing cards.

Mary kneeled down to look through them.

Suddenly she gasped. A shiver ran through her body. The one she held in her hand was a picture of the very man who had entered her bedroom in her vision.

And she thought she'd discovered the secret. This light-skinned ancestor had been a slave in an eastern state. He must have been born to a black slave-woman and her white plantation master.

Nineteen

AND SO CONTINUED MY YEARS among a people I had come dearly to love: 1974 through to the late 1980s.

I baptized their children and confirmed them. I confessed, communed, and married them. I preached weekly. Even the ones I had catechized grew up and had babies of their own.

When the publisher of my novel wanted me to spend a month touring the U.S., the church council said, "Yes," but only for portions of two weeks, always coming home to preach on the weekends.

I visited the sick. I sat by their beds, touched their brows with the sign of the cross, sang soft hymns in unhearing ears. I shoveled the snow from the church porch and the walks that went down to the street. Kneeling at the rail in the chancel, I prayed for the souls of the people whom God was pleased to place into my care. I cried out against the Devil who sought to oppress them. At their gravesides I spoke the words I knew by heart:

"We brought nothing into this world, and it is certain we can carry nothing out. The Lord gave, and the Lord hath taken away. Blessed be the name of the Lord. They that sow in tears shall reap in joy. . . ."

And I followed their young men to the courtroom and into their prison cells.

A YOUNG MAN NAMED Junie Piper was arrested for rolling a man in front of the police station.

Junie had the large, liquid eyes of a fawn. When I first met him in his mother's house and we shook hands, I came away wishing for a towel, so moist, so pliable was his handshake.

He had been dishonorably discharged from the Navy. In Evansville the poor fellow was at a loss. He roamed the streets. He would stand mutely among the gang that parked cars and boomed boxes and drank whiskey in front of the library. Junie hadn't the gumption to join the festivities—only to be present. If he looked for a job, I didn't know it.

And then he didn't even have the sense to do his crime in some dark alley. Cops saw the petty crime and arrested him immediately.

I visited him in jail.

There is little correcting in our correctional institutions. There is rather a stripping of identity—not only of the inmates, but also of their visitors.

In order to get to the second floor, where Junie was being held, you enter first the police office. You pick up a phone on which there is no dial. It rings upstairs. After a while someone might answer.

"Yes?"

"I've come to see Melvin Piper. I'm his pastor."

"Go to the elevator and wait."

The elevator too lacks buttons to signal up or down. You stand until the guard upstairs finds the time to open the door electronically.

You step into an austere cubical.

You wait.

Then the guard closes the door and the elevator groans to the second floor.

There you step out into a room of cinder blocks. To the left is a bank of cubbies into which you are to store whatever is in your pockets.

Across the room, behind a window with a speaking hole, guards keep their rifles and sit watching TV screens that monitor the halls and the cells.

You wear your clerical collar as evidence of your ministerial profession.

When he is ready, a guard says, "What?"

Once again you identify yourself and your reason

for coming: "I want to pray with Melvin Piper."

"Wait."

The guard disappears then reappears through a metal door. "This way."

He leads you down a grey hallway past the bars of small cells. Each cell is like a chamber in a beehive, one man inside: a bed attached to the left wall, a metal toilet at the back.

"Piper! Your preacher's here."

And there is Junie.

He lies on the floor wearing nothing but underpants. His head is close to the bars. His afro is flattened on one side and filthy.

I kneel near him.

"Junie?"

He lifts a vacant face, looks at me, then lays his head down on his arms.

"Junie," I say, "what are you doing in here?"

He doesn't answer. He doesn't speak.

So I am left to do all the talking.

"Your mother misses you. Do you want to see her?"

No answer.

I do the pastoral thing. I talk of the love of Jesus. Of forgiveness, whatever a judge might say, because Jesus is the only real judge. Does he know Jesus?

I spend fifteen minutes with this mute, and end my stay with a prayer, and leave unhappily.

This day, the next day, a week, two weeks—always

the same. I ask questions. He doesn't answer.

Then comes the day when Junie raises his head and says, "Can we talk?"

"Yes. Of *course*."

"Not here."

I run for the guard. I beg for a room and a table. The guard is gracious. He leads us to such a room and lets us in. "Ten minutes," he says. "Then I'll be back." He locks the door. I hear the crack of his heels as he walks away.

There is a table indeed and two chairs on either side of it.

We sit.

I lean forward to listen. Slowly, brokenly, he mumbles about his ruinous life in the Navy. He had been a cook. He thought he might find a job cooking for some restaurant in Evansville. But he was turned away and quit trying.

"Do you know how foolish it was to roll that man right in front of the police station?"

But he talks about his mother, Lola, and his sister. His speech softens. I can barely hear him. It trails off.

Silence.

I hear the guard's steps as he returns.

The guard knocks three times on the door.

Junie rises up terrified, as if a bomb has exploded.

He has to lean on me as we take him back to his cell.

But he has talked! He has talked to me!

Now when I visit him, I tell him a story.

"A man had two sons. One of his sons wanted his inheritance right now. His father gave it to him, and that son went off to join the Navy. It didn't occur to him that while he lived with his father his treasure was limitless. Soon he discovered that the inheritance was limited. It ran out, and he was left with nothing. No money, no friends, no dignity. Not even a name. He began to loathe himself because he thought he was worthless.

"He decided to go home again. But because he had come to nothing and had nothing to offer his father, he hoped at least that he could be a slave in his father's house.

"But Junie, Junie, his father had all along been sorrowful at the loss of his son.

"His father had been looking for him to come back, even standing on the roof of his house in order to see as far as he could.

"Then here came the boy, slouching up the road.

"And what did his father do then? Why, he jumped down and raced toward his son. And when he got there, he threw his arms around him and laughed and cried. He said, 'Let's have a party, because you were lost and I have found you again. You were dead and now you are alive.'

"Junie," I say. "Do you know who that father was? He was *your* father. And do you know who your father is? God. He is your *God*. And he loves you."

One day while I'm working at home, the telephone rings. It is a collect call for me. Will I accept the charges?

Yes.

Then I hear Junie's voice. He says, "Well."

Of course! You can't call from the prison on the prison's dime.

"Junie!" I say. "You got up! You even knew my number!"

He says, "Well."

"I am so proud of you," I chatter on. "Are you dressed? Have you showered? Are you better now?"

He says, "Well." And then he says, "I love you."

AND SO IT WENT at Grace. And so went my pastorate.

The fact that I had emerged from despair to faith gave me knowledge of Junie's despair, as well as the despair of the indigent.

Hence the fervor of my prayers.

I continued to publish books. Maybe Linda Hudson was the only person who actually read them. But the members altogether were proud that their pastor was building a reputation, for it was their reputation too.

The city came up with a plan to raze our neighborhood and gentrify the place. Grace fought the city to a standstill.

We enjoyed summer picnics.

I earned the right to slap the old black women on their backs.

When one mother who sat on the church council brought her infant to the meetings, the meetings became generous. That baby's presence caused conflicts to cease.

The church at large required its congregations to fill out regular forms: How many were baptized in that year? How many worshipped on a Sunday? And how many communicant members did the congregation have? How many joined that year?

Well, I could answer a number of questions, but I could not give an accurate account of those who worshipped and what the membership was—because so many people gathered with us who were *not* members, nor did I require membership of all who worshipped. We were more than a particular church of a particular synod. We were the children of our father, the merciful Lord God Almighty.

Twenty

WHERE NOW IS MY PAST? Where is the me that once was me, but is me no longer? In what things does that spirit lurk? And in what closets are sorted all the things I did and the feelings which once overwhelmed my world?

I am in the sixty-eighth year of my age. I left Evansville twenty-two years ago.

Where is my past. Is it somewhere still?

I think so.

Is it real still, and still powerful?

Yes. I think so.

My past is here, not gone at all. All its goodness and all its troubles, they are just beneath the surface of the present like fish under the surface of a green sea. And when the sea is undisturbed, the fish rise up again.

Not long ago I visited Grace Church, and the past rushed at me from a thousand hiding places. It has always been there, in the rooms themselves, the window, the shapes of the walls and shadows, in the sounds and the smells, in the corners and the colors.

I found myself simply standing in the sanctuary, alone, watching the past appear like clouds while the room grew dark and the evening fell.

All around me weddings spoke solemn vows, then laughed their exultations. Glad people fresh and smelling like flowers. And I am preaching.

All around me walk the slow procession of mourners, and a long succession of caskets, and if I look carefully into each, I can name the faces there, and sometimes relatives dab their eyes.

All around me run the children, both black and white, oblivious of colors, and they yank my robes and tell me secrets and love me and allow me to hug them. They are growing so fast that the infants I baptized stand as tall as I, and it is Sunday morning, and I am preaching.

These are real. My past is real.

It is in music and choirs and carols, and I stand wide-eyed, altogether entranced with the dark mystery of the God who is not gone at all, but is here and in my heart.

I am the various people I have been, careless and cocky and confident and scared. I am kneeling at my installment while the congregation sings in deep black voices. I am distributing the body of the Lord while the congregation sings, "Let us break bread together on our knees."

Who is Walt? Where is he?

In the music. In the air.

He is all the countless ghosts of his past.

And I am preaching.

Oh, how I labored over sermons, terrified that disciplinary words might hurt too much (or else have no effect at all). How assiduously I endeavored to teach the people—by writing, by speaking, by crying out, by example—the nature of God and the call of Christ, the absolutely necessary practice of forgiving one another.

Look: I am the child who enters the room where his father trimmed the Christmas tree.

I am the student, considering suicide.

I am the man translating Jerome's Latin Bible and landing on the verse in Galatians which calls him into the ministry.

I am the newlywed, walking with my wife out of the church and into a high wind which blows her veil like a ship's sail over her head.

I am the father, raising chickens.

And I am preaching.

My past is so heavily present that I can scarcely bear it. But I *am* my past.

The years of our lives are threescore and ten, or even by reason of strength, fourscore.

Grace Church, never, never will you not be in my heart. You are part of me, of all my five senses. Forever the imprint. Forever the love. Forever the past.

Walter Wangerin, Jr.
September 6, 2012

Also available from
RABBIT ROOM PRESS:

THE MOLEHILL VOL. 3
An Annual Journal by the Rabbit Room Community

THE WARDEN AND THE WOLF KING
Book 4 of the WINGFEATHER SAGA
by Andrew Peterson

BEHOLD THE LAMB OF GOD:
AN ADVENT NARRATIVE
by Russ Ramsey

THE WORLD ACCORDING TO NARNIA
by Jonathan Rogers

THE FIDDLER'S GUN and *FIDDLER'S GREEN*
by A. S. Peterson

REAL LOVE FOR REAL LIFE
by Andi Ashworth

SUBJECTS WITH OBJECTS
by DKM and Jonathan Richter

THE WILDERKING TRILOGY
by Jonathan Rogers

RABBIT ROOM
— PRESS —
NASHVILLE, TENNESSEE

www.RabbitRoom.com